D1531184

THE WAY A Revolutionary Curriculum

For further information and booking, please contact
Tim Timmons by visiting **www.TimTimmons.com**.

Copyright © 2016 by Tim Timmons
Published by Embers Press,
2618 San Miguel Dr., Newport Beach, CA 92660

The Way – A Revolutionary Curriculum
e-Book at **www.timtimmons.com**
Audio at **www.timtimmons.com**

ISBN-13: 978-0-9842429-3-1
e-Book ISBN-13: 978-0-9842429-8-6

The Way © Cover & Interior Design by Mark & Kim Seigler
Edited by Rick Kurjan

e-Book edition September 2016
Printed in the United States of America

All rights reserved. No portion of this book may be reproduced, stored in a retrieval system, or transmitted in any form or by any means – electronic, mechanical, photocopy, recording, scanning, or other – except for brief quotations in critical reviews or articles, without the prior written permission of the publisher. Unless otherwise identified, all Scripture quotations in this publication are taken from, the New American Standard Bible® (NASB), copyright © 1960, 1962, 1963, 1968, 1971, 1972, 1973, 1975, 1977, 1995 by The Lockman Foundation, used by permission. Other versions used include: the Holy Bible, New International Version® (NIV®). Copyright © 1973, 1978, 1984, 2011 by Biblica, Inc.® Used by permission of Zondervan. All rights reserved worldwide. www.zondervan.com. The "NIV" and "New International Version" are trademarks registered in the United States Patent and Trademark Office by Biblica, Inc.®; and THE MESSAGE (MSG), copyright © 1993, 1994, 1995, 1996, 2000, 2001, 2002, used by permission of NavPress Publishing Group.

1 2 3 4 5 6 7 / 21 20 19 18 17 16

THE WAY

VOLUME I: PERSONAL TRANSFORMATION

STUDY GUIDE 1: "SEE!"

STUDY GUIDE 2: "FOLLOW!"

THE WAY

STUDY GUIDE 1: "SEE!"

INTRODUCTION

STUDY GUIDE 1: "SEE!" contains 6 Study Sessions:

Study Session #1 - What Went Wrong?...The Problem!

Study Session #2 - What Went Wrong?...The Solution!

Study Session #3 - Jesus Is Good News for Everyone!

Study Session #4 - Jesus Is Life's Focal Point!

Study Session #5 - The End Game Is to Change You & Your World!

Study Session #6 - How to Experience the Presence of Jesus!

THE WAY is the first in a series of small group studies.

THE WAY includes 4 Study Guides, each with 6 Study Sessions. These 24 studies are not written in the traditional study guide format, with one person being the teacher and the rest listening. Instead, they are designed to promote discussion and interaction within the context of a few people gathered together. This is based upon the conviction that *"when two or three are gathered in the name of Jesus,"* Jesus will show up! This is a Jesus curriculum without political or religious agendas. His name is Jesus of Nazareth. We're not talking about the religious Jesus. We're talking about the most prominent and powerful person ever — just Jesus, simply the person of Jesus.

There's something about Jesus without religious baggage — his words, his Spirit, his actions, his loving ways, his bent toward the disenfranchised, and even his name — that brings healing and wholeness. Jesus is truly the most effective person you can embrace for yourself. The Jesus movement is the fastest growing movement in the world today within every culture!

THE WAY is not just another Bible study or a lecture from one to the many;

it is a revolutionary way for everyone to participate and SEE Jesus personally. The ultimate purpose of **THE WAY** small group curriculum is to participate in the Jesus movement for the transformation of nations through love — loving God, loving one another, loving others, and even loving your enemies. It's a revolution of love! The single-mindedness of **THE WAY** is to gather people together initially for personal transformation and then to change the world.

In the year 2002, a former communist, atheist guerilla fighter encountered Jesus while in political prison and found a new freedom. The same year, a former Christian pastor and author encountered Jesus while imprisoned by religiosity and was set free! ***THE WAY*** *contains the principles that transformed their lives and set them free!* ***THE WAY*** *is not the invention of two men; it is the plan and practice of Jesus from the very beginning!*

*Begin your Jesus journey with **THE WAY** and invite others to walk with you.*

WHAT WENT WRONG?...The Problem!

In our fast-paced world, life feels out of control.

All over the world, there are common concerns and common issues that are identified as the major problems – greed; crime; cruelty; corruption; extremism and terror; moral deterioration; racial, ethnic, and religious conflicts; intolerance, etc. Families are not stable. Relationships are not lasting. Most people are dissatisfied or, at least, uncertain about what is happening! The moral ground of right and wrong is shifting. It's more and more difficult to trust the governmental, religious, and corporate institutions. These concerns and issues are found in all the nations and communities without exception. They only vary in levels, scopes, or sophistications!

In our personal lives, we are unhappy. As a global society we have lost our way and desperately need to find the way back on track. We want to change our lives, our surroundings, and our nations. We want to make a difference in the world. We want peace, reconciliation, and social progress to prevail. But oftentimes we don't know the way. We tried many ways, but failed. Nothing seems to work. As a result, most embrace the herd mentality, because it's familiar and seems safe. The need to belong is stronger than the drive to dare to make a difference, so go along to get along becomes the theme. In summary, many things about our personal lives are wrong. Many things about our relationships are wrong and almost everything around the world is going wrong.

Let's further examine these in the following three areas: <u>Personal</u>, <u>Relational</u>, and <u>Global</u>.

 What things come to mind where you see that we have lost our way?

Where do you feel the most pressure to go along with the crowd to get along?

 How is your life working for you? Are you still trying to figure out how to live life to the fullest?

1. WHAT IS WRONG IN OUR PERSONAL LIVES

No matter our status in life — financial, relational, professional — there is only one thing that really matters: <u>Is our life working for us</u>? <u>Is what we are doing getting us what we really want</u>?

When life isn't working, and when a low-grade depression sets in as a result, where do we turn in times like these? What is it that we can hang on to, when we find ourselves saying, **"Why?" "Why me?"** or **"Why now?"** How do we obtain a sense of guidance?

The most natural thing to do is to blame something, anything, for what's not working. We may deeply blame ourselves. Or, better yet, it's easy to blame someone else for our predicament. And, when our lives aren't working, our lives are out of control, and when our lives are out of control, we will find ourselves in a swirl of fear, anger, guilt, shame, loss of purpose and destiny, hopelessness, worry.

 Who or what do you blame most often when things aren't going your way?

"FEAR"

When our future is out of control, we will have fear. Every day when we wake up, we are blasted with the message that there is something fearful out there or in our own minds that can harm us or bring inevitable disaster upon us.

To mention a few examples:
- We are afraid of dying and that it would be the end of our life.
- We are afraid of being sick and crippled and not being able to work or even to walk.
- We are afraid of losing our jobs for any reason.
- We are afraid of losing our money/wealth or the possessions we have and becoming poor.
- We are afraid of losing our loved ones.
- We are afraid of losing our power, our fame, and our "good" name.
- We are afraid of being responsible for our wrongdoing.
- We are afraid of a failure of harvest or a failure of our businesses.
- We are afraid of raising our children, not being able to send them to school, not being able to feed them three times a day, or not being able to pay bills . . . and so forth.

"ANGER"

When our present is out of control, we will have anger. People and circumstances just aren't doing what we want them to do and are out of control:

- The spouse or child who is out of control.
- The driver who just cut you off on the highway.
- The water heater that just blew up and your car that has broken down — again!
- The taxi or the bus or the train that is not on time.
- The health situation that is troubling.
- Questions as to how to get ahead and get out of being stuck in this situation.

In addition to the people and circumstances that are out of control, there is one more thing that continues to fuel anger in our minds. It might be called brain-chatter. Here is how it works. We tend to do the following: Expect the worse. Personalize everything. Live by the power of the "shoulds," shoulding ourselves to death. Specialize in mind-reading games, thinking we know what's really going on. Take in criticism and block out compliments. See everything in terms of black and white. Compare, compare, compare. Overgeneralize – always and never! Blame and attack. Insist that nothing be changed. We must always be right and never, ever wrong. Thinking this way is guaranteed to fuel our anger!

- We are not satisfied in our job or workplace or with our business.
- We are angry with ourselves, making the same mistakes every time.
- We have turmoil in us that we can't explain.
- We always think of bad things happening to us.
- We have negative thoughts and nightmares.
- We see ourselves as hated, neglected, cursed, etc.
- We are hurt, having had bad experiences we can't forget.

Anger occurs when we are frustrated with our present being out of control. Life just gets out of control no matter which way we turn.

"GUILT"

When our past is out of control, it's usually due to guilt. Dealing with our past can be so destructive. Most tend to dwell on the past so much that it becomes impossible to move forward. Some spend so much time focusing on the past that they just can't see anything else. They are stuck there. It's like having a rearview mirror that is larger than our windshield. We have to stick our heads out of our windows to see where we are going. Our past blocks the way of our present and our future, and that's dangerous!

- We feel guilty by what we did to others.
- We make ourselves guilty by what is happening or what happened to others.
- We feel guilty by our past actions that could have made our lives better today.

What must happen is to take the past out of our present and future and put it back into the past where it belongs. But this, in itself, is not enough. You see, we might think we are burying our past, but when we bury it alive, our past will nag and haunt us, working toward our destruction. Somehow we have to do something to put our past to death, and then our past will be under control.

The theme of being out of control continues! Fear appears when our future is out of control. Anger shows up when our present is out of control. And, guilt gnaws away at our gut when our past is out of control. All three of these render us paralyzed, damaged, and ineffective.

"SHAME"

There is a fourth kind of paralysis – shame. <u>Shame is the residue of having been seized by fear, anger, and guilt</u>. It manifests itself in a similar way as a low-grade infection – even a low-level depression. Shame is a contamination of your personness – <u>a blight that leaves you feeling inadequate or feeling not good enough</u>.

- We are ashamed of our past history.
- We are ashamed of our mistakes and/or crimes.
- We are ashamed of our addictions to alcohol, smoking, sex, gambling, stealing, lying, cheating. . . .
- We are ashamed of how we have misused our finances.

With shame it's not that our past, present, or future is out of control, but we are out of control; we are like a small boat that is being tossed about in a storm or a Ping-Pong ball that is being driven by the wind and once in a while experiences a hard hit. These four toxins are relentless enemies of people everywhere. No one is immune!

"HOPELESSNESS"

There is a fifth kind of paralysis that has gripped our world – hopelessness.
After holding to a belief that something "out there" can instantly fill up the emptiness inside and being disappointed again and again, a numbness sets in that craves greater and greater stimulation in order to make us feel alive. This inordinate craving leads to an anxious drive to go to extremes – extreme sports and adventures, bigger and better things, smaller yet faster technologies. These may be harmless by themselves and even have a genius of creativity, however none of these is therapeutic for the soul. This is a setup for addiction and obsessive behavior. The gnawing question continues, "When is enough, enough?"

It's different from having a <u>disease</u>. Instead of disease, it's being in a state of <u>unease</u> or generalized dissatisfaction with life. We crave satisfaction – a sense of security – yet most are finding themselves living in a state of perpetual dissatisfaction. After doing all we know to do or doing all "everybody" else is doing, there is a gnawing emptiness at the gut level. We're living with no sense of purpose – no meaning in life. As a young professional recently admitted, "There really does seem to be a hole in my soul that I can't fill."

When hopelessness reigns, the hole in the soul has a large opening and is ready for filling up with whatever or whoever is next. This has created a vast opening for young people to be drawn into self-centeredness, to accumulate wealth to feel better, and to strive after positions of power to gain self-importance. This same allurement sets them up to be recruited into drugs, pornography, sex-slavery, gangs, and both domestic and international terrorism. At all levels, hopelessness fills the heart!

 How have you tried to manage your fear, anger, guilt, and shame? Did it make them better or worse?

 How has self-reliance worked for you?

2. WHAT IS WRONG IN OUR RELATIONAL LIVES

In the same way we crave satisfaction and live in a state of dissatisfaction, we also crave intimacy yet experience a painful detachment – a gnawing ache of loneliness. Intimacy – everyone wants it, all shrinks talk about it, the movies sell it, the pornographers counterfeit it, the self-help books promise it, but very few actually experience it – it's so alluring and yet so elusive! The most frustrating aspect of the search for intimacy may be that you can't pursue it as a direct goal; you reach it only as the by-product of your genuine willingness to be open with yourself and with other human beings!

This painful detachment is a cold hollowness. The hollowness can be described as:

- The pain you suffer when you give love and love isn't reciprocated.
- The pain when love should have been there but wasn't from a parent, spouse, or friend.
- The pain of having an unhappy marriage.
- The pain when you are unappreciated and misunderstood.

- The pain of being loved wrongly (e.g. with material things, etc.).
- The pain of being deceived in love, due to lies and deception.
- The pain when you've loved and your love seemingly made no difference.
- The pain of betrayal by a spouse, dear friend, business partner, or boss.
- The pain of physical and emotional abuse.
- The pain of not being able to forgive or to seek forgiveness.
- The pain of a "friend" who seems to have a hidden agenda to use you rather than being a faithful friend who supports you.

 **What events or circumstances in your life have caused you the most emotional pain?**

Is your method for dealing with the pain helping to get rid of it or making it worse?

Because of this intense pain within relationships, there is a built-in self-destruction.

- We feel unsafe and unprotected in relationships and therefore are not free to be who we feel we are.
- We feel unsupported and abandoned, lacking team members.
- We feel a sense of inadequacy – a lack of confidence – even among our closest friends and family members.
- We tend to go deaf on relationships altogether.
- We don't view our relationships as part of our allies to make us stronger.

- We tend to view everyone as a competitor and therefore a threat to our success.
- We find it difficult to make lasting commitments. We prefer convenient relationships. We may be good in a crisis, but not so good in the continual.

Therefore, we settle for relationships that are held together by performance rather than the beautiful experience of unconditional love. Since we rarely experience such a thing, we aren't sure it even exists. Mother Teresa described this human condition well when she said, "The most terrible poverty is loneliness and the feeling of being unloved."

 What do you do, when you're alone?

 Do you have someone you can be with and talk with when you're hurting?

3. WHAT IS WRONG IN OUR VOLATILE WORLD

When we say our world we mean our workplace, our community, and the world at large.

- Is our workplace a place of happiness or a place of stress and dissatisfaction?
- Are we in the profession we like and believe that we are at the right place?
- Are we making a difference in and with our work?
- Are we working as a means of living, earning money, or as a value of life?
- What do our relationships look like with our fellow workers and with our boss?
- Do we know our neighbors?

- Are we befriended with our neighbors?

- Are we ready to help our neighbors in any way we can when they are in need?

- Who are we in our community?

- Do we do something worthwhile for the community?

- Do we have ideas for how to change the life of the community in a good way? How do we think of doing it?

- How do we think our community would benefit from our participation?

- What are the important needs in our community and what can we do together with others?

People were created to be valued and loved; things were created to be used. The reason the world is in chaos is because material things are being valued and loved, and people are being devalued and used. The result is that any hope of building true character is easily corrupted and loving, trusting relationships become an elusive dream.

We continue to crave satisfaction, yet we live in a state of dissatisfaction. We crave intimacy, yet we experience a painful detachment – a gnawing ache of loneliness. We also crave significance – to make a difference in this messed-up world. It seems the more we crave a sense of worth the more we are hit with disorientation and devaluation of our efforts. Discouragement replaces any optimism we have been able to collect. Our craving to make a difference is overwhelmed by massive confusion about what to do and how to do it.

We are bombarded with deterrents and distractions from every direction, all of which threaten every good intention we embrace.

- War is becoming even more an everyday phenomena between states, ethnic groups, religions, and peoples.

- Man's inhumanity to man is increasing to the most evil levels we've seen in modern times. We are witnessing inhuman practices against humans – kidnappings, beheadings, people burned alive in public cages, suicide bombings, etc.

- Natural disasters, earthquakes, and calamities are increasing.

- Poverty, famine, and disease are becoming rampant, threatening nations.

- Corruption in governments and businesses is widespread.

- Unemployment and under-employment are creating destabilization.

- Repression, bad governance, poor leadership and mismanagement, injustice, and crime are increasing.

- Political, religious, and ethnic conflicts are worsening every day.

- People are feeling more and more helpless and insecure.

Our noble cravings for satisfaction, intimacy, and significance are thwarted. We are left with broken hearts, broken spirits, broken bodies, broken homes, broken lives, and broken relationships. All in a broken world.

 How is your life busier, more complicated, more stressful, or more painful than ever?

 What is your response to the news and events that are happening around you or that you hear about happening somewhere else?

WHAT HAVE WE DONE TO GET THESE THINGS RIGHT?

In most of the things we face today, the only thing we can do is worry.

We see no way of making adequate changes, so we build up greater anxiety. This anxiety produces a profound frustration. It's a downward cycle of worry, frustration, more worry, anger, health issues, and more worry . . . it never ends and it's painful!

We do our best to handle the pain. At first most become experts in the art of denial that the problem or pain is not that bad. Or, the common denial is, "It's not that bad yet."

Denial only works for a time, until the pain becomes unbearable. This leads to a secondary move to handle the pain – to self-medicate! We handle the pain through medicating ourselves with alcohol, drugs, toys, and a variety of distractions. No matter how much we use and abuse, the medication works only temporarily.

In fact, we acquire new problems. We take on addictions to the medications. The very medication we choose to relieve the pain becomes monstrously destructive. This triggers another downward, depressive spiral.

We lie to ourselves as if we don't have any problem and continue suppressing and redefining the pain in hopelessness. We try to buy happiness with our money. In the end, all of these attempts to soothe the pain amount to putting Band-Aids on hemorrhages. We've concerned ourselves with our symptoms, but not with the source of our problems and pain.

Not even the highest levels of power in the world — social, military, political, and religious — have been able to produce a lasting solution to our personal, relational, and global troubles. Not even the most promising ideologies nor the most capable diplomacies have proven to be solutions to man's problems. No way has yet been universally identified.

 Here's the problem. There are three primary blockages as we search for the way to get our personal lives, our relational lives, our workplaces, our communities, our nations, and the world back on track.

FIRST: <u>Fundamentally flawed delivery systems</u>.

So far, the ways to solve these problems are political, diplomatic, religious, military, witchcraft, self-proclaimed philosophical thoughts, or psychological/psychiatric prescriptions. And these delivery systems are at best imperfect, and at worst, corrupt and defective. We've met with leaders in some of the worst regions of the world. The leadership soon tires of the failed attempts to make peace where there is no peace. The track record of failure creates a kind of numbness, accompanied by cynicism and hopelessness. What's interesting is that the proponents of these delivery systems incessantly show up to try and give people hope in a world that has been torn apart, or at least confused, by them. They posture their programs as saviors, yet prove out to be saboteurs. They are flawed by their inherent agendas, motivated by the same purpose of perpetuating their own existence. Their way leads to nowhere. <u>Reconciliation and peace cannot happen within this context</u>!

SECOND: A faulty starting point.

What we're talking about is bringing the power of making a positive difference into our society. Mahatma Gandhi, one of the all-time leaders in social change, saw this power clearly. He said it this way: "You must be the change you want to see in the world." No program, no matter how effective, has the power to bring change. Only changed people can affect change in society. You can't give away, teach, or mandate what you don't already own yourself. Why is it that the same program can produce dramatically different results? It may be the same program; it's the leadership dynamic that makes the difference. All positive change in society must start with you! Albert Einstein said, "No problem can be solved from the same level of consciousness that created it."

THIRD: A shallow strategy of reformation rather than transformation.

Reformation always sounds good and looks good, but it only has the power to reform — to rearrange the externals. People enthusiastically rally around reform programs. They are easy to embrace because they are easy to manage. The basic problem is that reformation traffics in symptoms without ever dealing with the source of the problem, therefore no authentic change occurs. Or, if there is perceived change, it's useless in making a significant difference in personal, relational, and global problems. In the end, reformation has the noble goal of rearranging the deck chairs on the Titanic. Transformation is what is needed at the core level — an inner change of heart — to see your life, your relationships, your workplace, your community, your nation, and the world differently.

 Have you been involved with any of these faulty systems or strategies? What were the results for you?

IN SEARCH OF THE WAY

<u>After examining and experiencing the limitations of the primary blockages of change we have come to the realization that inner transformation has to come from a spiritual "higher power."</u>

The most preferable higher power has the potential of being godlike. This is why those ways mentioned above can't work as adequate higher powers. They are man-made systems with so many add-ons that are governed by culture, man's interpretations of Holy Scriptures, emotional prejudices, historical traditions, and sacred opinions of mankind everywhere. Man-made systems are nothing more than systems of dos and don'ts — mostly don'ts!

<u>What is desperately needed is a relationship with the higher power — a personal relationship with a godlike entity that can change you and others on the inside.</u>

We have come to realize that there is <u>only one who qualifies as an adequate higher power</u>. <u>His name is Jesus</u>. We're not talking about the religious Jesus. We're talking about the most prominent and powerful person ever — just Jesus, simply the person of Jesus.

In the most pragmatic way, this Jesus seems to be able to affect these internal changes in people. We have experienced this personally and have observed this effect in people who need what he has.

There's something about Jesus without religious baggage — his words, his Spirit, his actions, his loving ways, his bent toward the disenfranchised, and even his name — that brings healing and wholeness to life. Jesus is truly the most effective person you can embrace for yourself.

Once an atheist, and a very closed-minded one at that, Oxford professor and critic C. S. Lewis became a follower of Jesus, reluctantly at first, by his own admission. But he saw enough of this winsome Jesus to take a halting step . . . one after the other, until at last he started thinking differently, living differently, teaching differently, and writing differently. He went from writing essays on literary criticism to writing *The Chronicles of Narnia*. And he remained a follower to the end of his life.

When Lewis was an atheist, he made the statement, "How absurd that a human could possibly believe that he could have a personal relationship with the Creator God." He said, "It is as absurd as Hamlet thinking he could have a personal relationship with Shakespeare, his creator." Later, on further thought, Lewis observed, "Hamlet could have had a personal relationship with Shakespeare, if Shakespeare had written himself, the author/creator, as a character into the play."

This is what we believe God did. He wrote himself into the play. The name of the character is Jesus.

"Come & See!"

Consider this Jesus who is revered as

- The **Christ** to Christians

- A **Rabbi** to the Jews

- A **Prophet** to the Muslims

- An **Avatar** to the Hindus

- An **Enlightened One** to Buddhists

- A **wise teacher** to secularists

- A **friend** to the broken and disenfranchised

However they view him, however you view him, his name is Jesus. And he is out to deliver the message of good news to all people of all religions — even to those with no religion at all — the way, the truth, and the life of all people.

People all around the world are eager to come and see . . . Jesus. And when you show them just Jesus, without all the cultural and ecclesiastical add-ons, they are drawn to him.

Come and see. Come and see this man who can't be explained, can't be put into a box, can't be categorized, systematized, or made religious. It doesn't matter where you are from — Europe or Africa, America or Asia or any other region. It doesn't matter who you are — male or female, King, President, General, laborer, or unemployed. It doesn't matter what you do — tax collector, fisherman, cleaner, housemaid, engineer or scientist or prostitute. It doesn't matter if you are a Sheikh, a High Priest, a Patriarch, an Arch Bishop, a centurion who pledges allegiance to Caesar, a pagan who offers sacrifices at the temple of Artemis, or a Pharisee who is part of a corrupt religious system.

Politics isn't the way….

  Religion isn't the way….

    Wealth isn't the way….

      Fame or celebrity isn't the way….

      War or violence isn't the way….

        THE WAY is Jesus! The only way!

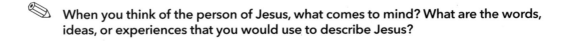

When you think of the person of Jesus, what comes to mind? What are the words, ideas, or experiences that you would use to describe Jesus?

Have you viewed Jesus as a revolutionary or just a religious leader?

Is there any good reason why you wouldn't follow after this Jesus and join the spiritual revolution to change yourself and then the world?

 If the religious ideas about Jesus were taken away from him, would that make it easier or more difficult for you to relate to him?

WHAT WENT WRONG?...The Solution!

WHAT IS SMALL GROUP?

Jesus is THE WAY. He is the ultimate answer to the question "What went wrong?" Many, no matter their religious or cultural backgrounds, are initially attracted to the person of Jesus, however, few experience the personal transformation only Jesus performs. Many become like parrots who can repeat the right answers and even reform their behavior to a degree, yet they have never experienced what it means to be changed from the inside-out — to be transformed. It's one thing to know a lot about Jesus, yet quite another to know Jesus personally — really! Jesus can be embraced and experienced through the supernatural dynamic of small groups. It's the power of the few.

 What are some things you know about Jesus?

 What has been your experience in being part of a small group? What was its purpose?

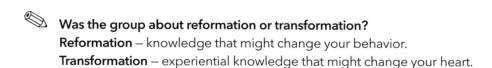 **Was the group about reformation or transformation?**
Reformation – knowledge that might change your behavior.
Transformation – experiential knowledge that might change your heart.

How did the group make a difference in your life?

What part of the world around you was changed because of your small group experience? What parts did you want to change, but could not?

The concept and practice of small groups is first established by God in his creation and then implemented in the form of a dynamic movement by Jesus in the process of the formation of his *ecclesia* – "cabinet" or called-ones – for the purpose of his Kingdom on earth, which essentially is transformation through the revolution of love.

However, in the development of the church over a few centuries, <u>the meaning and substance of the small group movement changed to mass meetings and assemblies of people</u>. Then, with the changing of the ecclesia to the big, organized "Church," the very existence and dynamic of small groups vanished from the community of believers in Jesus. Also, the idea of simply following Jesus morphed into being converted into a religious system known as "Christianity." Small, participatory groups were exchanged for larger, spectating assemblies.

When the use of small groups as the key way of following Jesus was eliminated from the Church, the secular world took it, gave it different names like "cell group," "team," "unit," "quality circle," "cabinet," "leadership model," "empowerment," "organism structure," etc., and used it for economic, government, business, military and other purposes. Communists took the small group model from Jesus and used it as an effective tool of making revolution in order to change social systems. Crime and terrorist groups use it for their evil purposes, too.

<u>Most of the present-day Churches are pursuing different forms of groups devoid of the real meaning, purpose, and substance of the original small groups</u>. They use it only as a program or technique of ministry rather than a call to return to the roots of the way of Jesus. The operational purpose of small groups in most Churches today is for building their numbers. To most, the small group strategy is the key to Church growth. Most of the current small group activities in Churches are dynamic techniques, rather than for the purpose of personal and people transformation. On the other hand, some Churches and many followers of Jesus have realized the nature and significance of small groups and are doing their best to use them effectively.

<u>Small groups are reflective of the very nature of God and humanity as community</u>. <u>Transformational small groups flow out of creation, resonating a harmonious chord of unity among the many differences within the cultures of the world</u>.

A small group is a voluntary and intentional gathering of 3 to 12 people, who meet regularly with a shared purpose.

<u>It is a gathering of a few persons to be, to share, and to act for the betterment of one another (loving one another) and for the good of others (loving your neighbor)</u>.

The general thesis is that <u>God has set in motion from the beginning certain divine and human realities that are uniquely imaged and reflected where a small number of persons come</u>

together. Within the dynamic of small group God's powerful and mysterious presence becomes evident. Jesus assured his followers, **"Where two or three gather together in my name, I will show up among you."**

The ultimate purpose of small group is to participate in the movement of the Kingdom of Jesus for the transformation of nations through love — loving God, loving one another, loving others, and even loving your enemies. It's a revolution of love!

CHARACTERISTICS OF SMALL GROUP

The single-mindedness of small group is to gather people together initially for personal transformation and then for these transformed lives to see their destiny to become agents of God to change the world by changing their surroundings. The small group exists for transformation!

Small group is about the interpersonal connections between two or more persons to have a common, intimate, and interconnected life — "doing life together." It is the process of very different, individual persons coming together into unity and oneness. It's the answer to the prayers of Jesus: **"That they may be one as we are one — I in them and you in me — so that they may be brought to complete unity"** (John 17:22-23, NIV) . **"Your kingdom come, your will be done, on earth as it is in heaven"** (Matthew 6:10, NASB).

Small group is not a program or a technique of ministry. It is a call to the roots of the very nature of what God created humanity to be. It is the practical meaning of the work of Jesus — ecclesia. Small group is a generic form of *human relationship* that is transcendent of gender, culture, religion, denomination, race, or any other classification.

The whole structural substance of small group is in loving relationships. This relational dynamic is in triplicate — your relationship with God, your relationships with one another within the group, and your relationships with those outside the small group. People come together and strive for intimate and lasting relationships of loving one another, for unity and for the experience of peace. In essence, small group is the substance of the family, the nucleus of community and of society.

Small group is the main means of making disciples (followers of Jesus) in all nations. All other means like preaching, evangelizing, crusading, conferencing, etc., are only secondary and supplementary. Making disciples is not about passing on information; it's about personal and people transformation!

As you can see, small group is so much more than a "Bible study." Small group is the primary way of transforming personal life and making a difference around us in the family, in the community, and in the society.

A small group can and must be multiplied and grow into a network of small groups. It is the fastest way to spread the good news of love and to change our surroundings and to change the world.

A small group can start anywhere and multiply. It can be fitted in urban as well as rural dwellings, in slums as well as in mansions and palaces, in workplaces, in government offices, in schools and colleges, in military camps, in religious institutions, and in media and entertainment institutions, etc. It is the best way to reach people anywhere they live, under any circumstances, in any context.

JESUS AND SMALL GROUP

Jesus began his movement to change the world by using the small group model as the manifestation of his cabinet and the principal way of discipleship. **He didn't come into the world to build another political or religious organization** (not even the religion known as Christianity).

His strategy was to call human beings into relationship with himself and with one another. His methodology was the establishment of small groups. Jesus didn't found an organization; he launched a movement in response to his challenging invitation: *"Follow me!"* As individuals move out with a few others to follow in the steps of Jesus, the movement begins.

Jesus changed human history through the process of forming an intentional small group. He began with only three and grew it to twelve young men, mostly teenagers. The diverse small group around Jesus gives a clear signal as to how God desires humanity to move within his Kingdom. Jesus could have chosen to rally the masses to come along with him, but he remained within the power of the few. The small group way is the Kingdom way of living life most successfully and effectively.

The focus of his ministry was to transform the mind, the heart, and the life of his followers, making disciples through small groups. He taught and preached in the synagogues and to multitudes of people in different venues. **But he invested most of his time in teaching and training, fellowshipping, praying and breaking bread with his small group.**

Contrary to the world's system, the goal of Jesus' small group (cabinet) was relational between the group and God and among themselves; it was neither program nor activities nor organization or institution nor structure or hierarchy. He lived and shared life within the small group, loved them, served them, and by way of serving became their leader, gave himself totally for them, and trained them to be and to do exactly what he was doing with them.

The finished work of Jesus is often attributed to his death on the cross, where he said, *"It is finished."* It is true that the sacrificial death of Jesus was astounding for so many reasons, however, Jesus, in his own words, explains what he believed his work on earth was to be. Jesus believed he finished the work God gave him to do by working with a few young men. He invited them into a small group dynamic where they experienced personal transformation, and he gave them the revolutionary purpose to multiply this transformational message to the world.

 From this section of John 17 above, how would you describe Jesus' purpose while he was on earth? What were his plans for his disciples?

Jesus demonstrated through his small group what the Kingdom of God in action, "on earth as it is in heaven," means and how the power of the few under his leadership are able to change the course of history.

The small group of Jesus existed in juxtaposition to the environment and culture of the society. The small group played several roles in the world. Jesus identified three of these roles in the images of **salt, light,** and **leaven**.

SALT

Jesus says to his followers, *"You are the salt of the earth!"*

Salt was used as a preservative to counteract the decay in meat. In order for the salt to be effective it must be out of the saltshaker and applied to the meat. Salt is the invisible presence of God. It must be sensed! The dynamic nature of a revolutionary small group is that each follower in the group is the invisible presence of God among those touched. Just think of the powerful, quiet presence that emanates from the power of the few as the salt of the earth. The presence of salt on the earth is the loving and powerful Kingdom presence of Jesus that counteracts the decay of the earthly kingdom. The core of salt can be found in learning to love God with all your heart, mind, body, and strength.

LIGHT

Jesus says, *"You are the light of the world!"*

Salt has a powerful invisible nature to it; light has more of the visible presence of God. Salt must be sensed – light must be seen! Light counteracts the darkness. The visible presence of God consists of the energy of salt and the expression of light. Just think of the authentic, attractive presence of light that emanates from the power of the few as the light of the world. The presence of the light of the world is the loving and powerful Kingdom presence of Jesus that counteracts the darkness of the earthly kingdom. The core of light can be found in loving your neighbor as yourself.

LEAVEN

Jesus says, *"The Kingdom of heaven is like the leaven*

[yeast] *a woman used in making bread. Even though she put only a little leaven in three measures of flour, it permeated every part of the dough."* The revolutionary small group of Jesus carries the leaven – the Good News of the Kingdom – and has the power to transform the whole system of life.

Jesus used living together with the small groups to transform the characters of his followers and change their way of life. He used his small group first to change the Twelve before he sent them to change the world. He first called his cabinet to follow him, then his small group was mandated to make followers of him in every nation, by the use of small groups. This pattern continues to replicate itself until society changes. It's irreversible like leaven!

THE EARLY FOLLOWERS OF JESUS

Early followers of Jesus followed his pattern and continued the small group model, which were called "house churches." Even though they preached in the temple courts and in synagogues, their main focus was small groups. Temples and synagogues (public places) were secondary. The center stage was always small groups (house churches). This was the essence of the early Jesus movement!

Until the third century AD (for over 300 years) there was no construction of buildings called Churches. The church was cell groups/house churches. Even after that period, it was the Roman Emperor who started constructing buildings that were called Churches.

Therefore, the meaning of church was changed to refer to a building. The word church has nothing to do with any kind of a building. The church, meant by Jesus as ecclesia, is not a religious word nor even a "Christian" word. It designates a group of people for a certain purpose. The church of Jesus is not a place to go; it's all about being the church and not going to Church.

WHAT DID THE SMALL GROUPS DO?

They shared the teachings of Jesus, they shared fellowship, they shared meals, they prayed and worshipped, they supported one another in their lives, and they loved one another in the love of Jesus.

They did not live for money or power or fame and popularity. They didn't build pedestals from which to pontificate. They demonstrated commitment and loyalty to Jesus. They were followers of Jesus who put him first before everything else. They saw everything through the eyes of Jesus.

They did not build fences or boxes around them to isolate themselves from the world. They were out to change the world. They interfaced with the world's systems of life to reach out with the Kingdom message. They reached out to the poor, to leaders and government officials, to different cultures, to different religions with only one message about a person. His name is Jesus.

Their purpose of life was to love Jesus and to love others. Love was the bond between them. Their center – their cornerstone – was nothing but Jesus. Their sole leader was Jesus and leadership of the cell groups was achieved by being servants.

There was no organization, hierarchy of power, denomination, or any kind of institutional setup. It was all lived out in the context of relationship. The Jesus movement was all about loving relationships – one on one and two by two.

Small group is the primary component to the revolutionary Jesus movement – the revolution of love. AND, THE REVOLUTION IS STILL ON TODAY!

✎ In your experience, how do small groups (though helpful) tend to fall short of the transformational model Jesus intended?

1.

2.

3.

4.

✎ Why do you think so many small groups might fall short of Jesus' model?

✎ Do you see how the small group dynamic of Jesus can be life changing for you and the world around you?

Who are the people God is giving you to share life with?

 What are you teaching and learning from each other?

JESUS IS GOOD NEWS FOR EVERYONE!

Throughout the Scriptures there was a great anticipation of God's Messiah,

God's anointed one. Messiah was a title for the King who was to experience the sign of **"the Spirit of the Lord mightily coming upon him."** This special anointing of the Spirit of God first came upon Jesus at his baptism by John, then the Spirit led Jesus into 40 days of testing and temptation in the wilderness, and now here Jesus returns to Galilee under the power of the Spirit.

It's in his hometown of Nazareth that Jesus aligns himself with the mission of proclaiming the Good News message to the world. This is the message of God's Messiah. You may be a little surprised as to what the Good News actually is. Let's visit that fascinating scene.

"And Jesus returned to Galilee in the power of the Spirit, and news about Him spread through all the surrounding district. And He began teaching in their synagogues and was praised by all." (Luke 4:14-15, NASB)

After being initially anointed by the Spirit of God, Jesus came back to his home region at the northern end of the Sea of Galilee. The response was overwhelmingly positive to what Jesus taught and what Jesus did with those who came to him. Over and over it was said that the people were amazed. It was inevitable and greatly anticipated that Jesus was at some point going to visit his home synagogue where he grew up.

He showed up at the synagogue in Nazareth, not as one of the crowd, but as a visiting "Rabbi." Whenever a Rabbi visited a synagogue, he was always asked to do something. The most common request was to read the Scriptures that were already set up and perhaps make some comments, explaining the reading. The readings were most always from the Five Books of Moses (the Torah) or the Prophets. (On three occasions I've been asked to read the Scriptures when I've visited a synagogue. It's a very long tradition.)

"And He came to Nazareth, where He had been brought up; and as was His custom, He entered the synagogue on the Sabbath, and stood up to read. And the book of the prophet Isaiah was handed to Him. And He opened the book and found the place where it was written,

> *"The Spirit of the Lord is upon Me,*
>
> *Because He anointed Me to preach the gospel to the poor.*
>
> *He has sent Me to proclaim release to the captives,*
>
> *And recovery of sight to the blind,*
>
> *To set free those who are oppressed,*
>
> *To proclaim the favorable year of the Lord."* (Luke 4:16-19, NASB)

The reading on this Sabbath was a Messianic passage from the prophet Isaiah. It was very explicit in articulating the Good News the "anointed" one, the one who has the Spirit of the Lord come upon him, would come to announce.

In the traditional move of respect, Jesus stood up to read the Scriptures before the congregation. Then, he sat down to make his comments.

"And He closed the book, gave it back to the attendant and sat down; and the eyes of all in the synagogue were fixed on Him. And He began to say to them, 'Today this Scripture has been fulfilled in your hearing.' And all were speaking well of Him, and wondering at the gracious words which were falling from His lips; and they were saying, 'Is this not Joseph's son?' " (Luke 4:20-22, NASB)

What Jesus is saying here for the first time publicly is that this announcement that was to come from the lips and life of God's Messiah was TODAY being fulfilled in their midst. In other words, Jesus is laying claim to being the one who has the Spirit of the Lord upon him and was sent as God's Messiah. It's quite clear! So, was it a coincidence that this passage to be read at the synagogue that Sabbath was this very specific Messianic message of Good News? I think not!

Let's examine again:

> *"The Spirit of the LORD is upon Me,*
>
> *Because He anointed Me to preach the gospel [Good News] to the poor.*
>
> *He has sent Me to proclaim release to the captives,*
>
> *And recovery of sight to the blind,*
>
> *To set free those who are oppressed,*
>
> *To proclaim the favorable year of the LORD."*

NOTE the elements of God's Good News. There are two announcements of Good News to specific groups. The first is to proclaim the Good News to the poor. The poor live in a state of tough circumstances and struggle and are used to bad news, however the Messianic message is precisely given to these disenfranchised people. The second announcement of Good News is to proclaim the favorable year of the Lord. This was the miraculous, a message filled with grace and mercy that happened every 50 years. It was known as the year of jubilee and celebration. It was a major new beginning for those in debt – a restart every 50 years. This Messianic proclamation seems to imply that every year is a time for everyone to start over and not be weighed down by your circumstances . . . that's Good News.

Then there are two announcements of freedom. The first is the proclamation to set prisoners free. Those who were in bondage can now live as free men and women. This is a primary Kingdom message brought by the Messiah. The second proclamation of freedom is to set all who are oppressed free. Again, you may be living in this earthly kingdom, oppressed from many directions and by many abuses and addictions. The Messiah and his Kingdom are giving everyone who wants it a new kind of freedom right here, right now, in the Kingdom of heaven.

> *The pinnacle of this Messianic passage and the claim to the Messianic mission is the "recovery of sight to the blind." The Messiah is to announce recovery of sight to all who are blind. This is not just physical blindness, but spiritual blindness – for everyone!*

The people of his hometown synagogue were so impressed and even shocked. He knew what they must be thinking and quickly addressed their obvious thoughts.

"And He said to them, 'No doubt you will quote this proverb to Me, "Physician, heal yourself! Whatever we heard was done at Capernaum, do here in your hometown as well." ' And He said, 'Truly I say to you, no prophet is welcome in his hometown.' (Luke 4:23-24, NASB)

Jesus knew they were eager to see for themselves the miracles that had been reported while he was in Capernaum, yet he also respects the principle that prophets are not well received at home. Then, Jesus shocks the congregation with two references as to how God's Good News and grace were experienced among the non-Jewish communities in years past. This was not music to the ears of this little Jewish congregation. Immediately after Jesus identifies himself as the one whom the Spirit of God had anointed, which is in line with their Jewish thinking, he first refers to the time of Elijah:

"But I say to you in truth, there were many widows in Israel in the days of Elijah, when the sky was shut up for three years and six months, when a great famine came over all the land; and yet Elijah was sent to none of them, but only to Zarephath, in the land of Sidon, to a woman who was a widow." (Luke 4:25-26, NASB)

During the great famine, God didn't send Elijah to the Jewish community, but to a widow in Zarephath, who was a Gentile — outside of the Jewish community. Here within this little closed Jewish community, proud of being God's people and filled with pride that they alone were the people of God's blessing, they had to wonder what Jesus was really saying.

Then Jesus turns to another illustration, making the same point:

"And there were many lepers in Israel in the time of Elisha the prophet; and none of them was cleansed, but only Naaman the Syrian." (Luke 4:27, NASB)

The prophet Elisha had the opportunity to heal the many lepers during his time and none of them were cleansed, with the exception of one man. His name was Naaman, who was from Syria.

So, the prophet Elijah was helped by a non-Jewish widow and the prophet Elisha healed only one leper . . . and he was a non-Jew. The awesome point of the Good News announcement is that the best news of all is that the Messianic Good News is for everyone, no matter their cultural or religious background and affiliation.

This is awesome news for the entire world, but it's not-so-good news to those who believe they exclusively own God and his blessings for themselves. This kind of inclusiveness threatens the very existence of a narrow belief system.

Now, **NOTE** what their response was to Jesus. It all started out so well with agreeing smiles and nods, but then turned quickly into rage.

"And all the people in the synagogue were filled with rage as they heard these things; and they got up and drove Him out of the city, and led Him to the brow of the hill on which their city had been built, in order to throw Him down the cliff. But passing through their midst, He went His way." (Luke 4:28-30, NASB)

This same kind of exclusive thinking is alive and well today throughout the world! This is the source of all kinds of jealousies, strife, and divisiveness.

The power of the Good News God's Messiah is to proclaim is not only directed toward the poor, those needing freedom from captivity and oppression, and giving sight to all kinds of blindness. The awesomeness of the Good News is that it is for everyone!

 Can you relate to the natural tendency for people to buy into exclusivity?

 How natural it is to believe that you are right and others are wrong? Or, that you are more right than others?

What has been your definition of the Good News or Gospel of God? What does it mean to you? What is it?

 What if Jesus, just Jesus, is the Gospel – the Good News of God? How does that feel to you? Does it make good sense to you?

In addition to the Nazarene synagogue experience where Jesus identified himself with the Good News message of the expected Messiah, later Jesus responds to John's questions in *Luke 7:20-23*:

"When [John's disciples] came to Him, they said, 'John the Baptist has sent us to You, to ask, "Are You the Expected One, or do we look for someone else?" ' At that very time He cured many people of diseases and afflictions and evil spirits; and He gave sight to many who were blind. And He answered and said to them, 'Go and report to John what you have seen and heard:

> *the blind receive sight,*
>
> *the lame walk,*
>
> *the lepers are cleansed,*
>
> *and the deaf hear,*
>
> *the dead are raised up,*
>
> *the poor have the gospel preached to them,*
>
> *Blessed is he who does not take offense at Me.' "* (NASB)

 What is the meaning of each of these today in your world?

Jesus wants his followers to fully represent or re-present him — to be Jesus to those in need. **NOTE** what Jesus said about himself: *"I am the Light of the world; he who follows Me will not walk in the darkness, but will have the Light of life"* (John 8:12, NASB).

NOTE what Jesus said about his followers: *"You are the light of the world. A city set on a hill cannot be hidden; nor does anyone light a lamp and put it under a basket, but on the lampstand, and it gives light to all who are in the house. Let your light shine before men in such a way that they may see your good works, and glorify your Father who is in heaven"* (Matthew 5:14-16, NASB).

So, how are you to be the light of the world – to be Jesus to others?
Could it be that you are to be Jesus to the same people Jesus came to touch?

<u>SO, who are these people in your life</u>?

the blind receive sight...
the lame walk...
the lepers are cleansed...
and *the* deaf hear...
the dead are raised up...
the poor have the Gospel preached to them...

Every time the question is asked, "What's the Gospel?"a myriad of answers are offered. Years ago, we asked a group of a few hundred people in a teaching session, "What is the Gospel?" As they called out their answers, there were 14 "definite" answers to the question "What is the Gospel?" The conclusion of our group was that it's no wonder that the world is so confused about the Gospel.

One organization that specializes in "evangelizing" children responded to our question with "It's complicated, because there are lots of dimensions to it." And, no one in the leadership of the organization could articulate what the many dimensions are. We need to get over our clichéd responses and accept the simplicity and purity of Jesus. **He is the Gospel – the Good News – simply Jesus.**

 What have you been taught the Gospel (Good News) is? What do you tell others the Gospel is?

WHAT IS THE GOSPEL (GOOD NEWS)?

The Gospel is not complicated and there are not many dimensions to it. The Gospel is good news to everyone! The Gospel is not a set of instructions, a series of multi-faceted dimensions, or even specific behaviors to follow. The Gospel is a person. His name is Jesus, simply Jesus!

When Jesus shows up, no one is the same again. Jesus, the revolutionary, brings the Good News for anyone who wants it.

- The dead are brought back to life.
- The blind see.
- The lame walk.
- The deaf hear.
- The mute talk.
- The sick are healed.
- The broken hearted are comforted.
- Enemies and rivals are reconciled to become friends.
- Women's status is elevated.
- The poor are made rich.
- The rich realize their poverty.
- The lost are found.
- The weak find strength.

No transformation is more vivid than what happened to the early disciples. They were weak-willed and timid, then found inner strength and courage. The usual reason given for this dramatic life-change is the resurrection of Jesus from the dead. The Resurrection is no doubt paramount, however we see their transformation coming from something else. Jesus spent 40 days with the disciples, where he spoke to them about the Kingdom of God. Here's what is said by Luke:

"To these He also presented Himself alive after His suffering, by many convincing proofs, appearing to them over a period of forty days and speaking of the things concerning the kingdom of God." (Acts 1:3, NASB)

Why did Jesus hang out with his early followers for 40 days after the Resurrection?

1.

2.

 Why was each so important?

The real transformation took place during the time spent with Jesus, eating and drinking and discussing principles of the Kingdom of God. And, this is the same today. When two or three are gathered together in the name of Jesus, he will show up and make a significant difference in all who have eyes to see and ears to hear him.

Now, here's the point. If Jesus brings positive transformation – the Good News – into every life he encounters, then doesn't it make sense for us to introduce everyone we can to this Jesus? You see, when Jesus shows up, no one is ever the same again!

GOSPEL OF THE KINGDOM

NOTE that when the people tried to keep him in one place, Jesus said, ***"I must proclaim the good news of the kingdom of God to the other towns also, because that is why I was sent"*** *(Luke 4:43, NIV).*

Jesus is the Gospel – Jesus, plus nothing else. Now, here Jesus talks about the "Gospel of the Kingdom." Jesus is the person (the what) of the Gospel. The Gospel is a person, not a program. And, the Kingdom of God is the way we act out this person's presence in our lives (the how). When you practice Kingdom principles, you are practicing the rule of Jesus in your life in that situation, in that moment. Wherever the King is, there is the Kingdom.

So, <u>the Gospel – the Good News – is Jesus and his Kingdom</u>. Seek first his Kingdom and his righteousness (that's Jesus). This is seen in the book of Acts. The primary theme is Jesus and the Kingdom. Jesus, in person, taught the disciples about the Kingdom. Jesus, in person, with his great I AM's, taught mostly about the Kingdom. Then at the end of Acts Paul hosts all those who are interested in his rented quarters and taught them about Jesus and the Kingdom of God. Jesus is the best Good News in the midst of this bad news world.

When you encounter Jesus, you will be changed or will be healed. The healing touch of Jesus' presence is most powerful and empowering, no matter your background or religious beliefs. So, do everything you can do to stay close with Jesus and his Kingdom and you will know his healing touch on your life. This is not just a first century experience; it is for today – for us and those we love.

WHEN DOES JESUS SHOW UP AS THE GOOD NEWS?

Think of it in this way. Jesus doesn't make appointments with you, therefore Jesus is always an interruption. Interruptions are never anticipated and can never be counted on, therefore interruptions are rarely pleasant and positive. They are, in fact, interruptions!

 List typical interruptions in your life where Jesus might be involved.

 Are your interruptions usually good news or bad news?

If Jesus is involved in the interruption, then is that good news or bad news?

No matter how bad the interruption, Jesus is up to something!
That's good news! Jesus is up to something special!

 If Jesus, just Jesus, is the Gospel – the Good News of God – then in order for you to receive the Good News of God into your life, what must you do?

JESUS IS UNIVERSAL

By "Jesus is universal," we mean that Jesus will work with anyone, anywhere. God is calling people to himself within every culture of the world. This was God's plan all along! This is why the Jesus movement is functioning all over the world today.

We have not met anyone who rejects Jesus. They may reject a poor caricature of him, but not Jesus. Some people may not accept Christianity, but they do not reject Jesus. Even the most popular books by atheists who claim to reject God are really rejecting the religious expressions of God. Jesus is altogether different! He is transcendent of religion, philosophy, or worldview.

Jesus is here for anyone and everyone, no matter their cultural, religious, or philosophical backgrounds. ***"For God so loved the world"*** is exactly what it means – the entire world. He didn't love a segment of the world. <u>Jesus is for everyone and will work with anyone</u>. No one has to be left behind, unless he wants to be. All those who want to come to Jesus can do so. Now, don't get us wrong, we're not saying all roads lead to Jesus. We're saying Jesus leads to all roads! There's a big difference!

JESUS IS FOR ANYONE

In the past few years we've been assured that there are millions of Hindus who are worshiping and studying about Jesus in homes in India. We're also witness of more and more Buddhists who are becoming devoted followers of Jesus. The Hindu Scriptures, written over 700 years before Jesus, clearly refer to the coming one. <u>These have been unthinkable thoughts, until now</u>! **Jesus is truly for everyone!**

Agnostics are another group of people who have many in their ranks who follow Jesus. In our experience they are perhaps the most open to Jesus when presented without all the religious baggage. Agnostics have a vacuum in their hearts. In my experience, this seems to be a God-shaped vacuum. I continually enjoy conversing with agnostics, once I am able to convince them that I don't want to discuss religion. It seems that this group is better able to view Jesus separated from the religious wrappings. They've already rejected the religious trappings and were left empty. **But, when introduced to Jesus without religious baggage, so often they respond by saying, "I can follow this Jesus!"**

The "self-help movement" is another group of people who revere Jesus, some going so far as to follow him. Though they may not use his name, they do use his teachings and his example.

Yes, Jesus plus nothing – <u>Jesus without religious baggage or boxes is attractive and can be satisfying for everyone everywhere</u>. Deadly narratives are spoken in the Christian, Muslim, and Jewish arenas that continue to stir up the deepest fears within the best people. These fears fuel ugly responses that divide our world. <u>Deadly narratives are formulated out of ignorance</u>!

There are Muslims and Orthodox Jews in the world who love and follow Jesus, but you might be unable to accept this thought. <u>Jesus unites and everything else divides, but unless you experience this uniting dynamic, it's difficult to get your brain around it</u>!

Looking at the long history of Jewish thought, some of the most prominent rabbis have come to revere Jesus as possibly the most influential Jew who ever lived. Dr. David Flusser, in his book ***The Sage From Galilee: Rediscovering Jesus' Genius***, broke down many barriers that have kept Jews from studying Jesus. Albert Einstein, one of the greatest scientists in the world, said this about Jesus: "<u>As a child I received instruction both in the Bible and in the Talmud. I am a Jew, but I am enthralled by the luminous figure of the Nazarene. No one can read the Gospels without feeling the actual presence of Jesus. His personality pulsates in every word</u>."

Meanwhile, most Christians are unaware that the Muslim holy book, the **Qur'an,** refers to Jesus more times than it does Muhammad. The prophet Jesus, known as Isa, is held up as the only supernatural prophet. The prophet Jesus is presented as a miracle worker, the **"Word of God,"** the **"clear sign of God,"** born of a virgin, alive today, and coming back to bring peace on earth. Jesus is viewed as the unique One, who was articulated in the Injil (the Gospels of the Bible). But when Muslims attempt to study the life and teachings of Jesus, they do so with the weight of history against them, too. The ugly history of the Crusades still lingers today. Add to this ugliness the hateful narrative from extremists within the Christian and Muslim communities, and you can see why Jesus' image has become so distorted in many Muslims' eyes. Today we received an email from a friend who says that a number of his colleagues in ministry in Muslim countries now estimate that "Muslim born again followers of Jesus outnumber those who are born again believers from a Christian background."

In many ways this is nothing new. <u>Jesus has always worked with people from every culture and found them to be attracted to him</u>. The problem in the first century was the religious jealousy of the "gate-keepers" of Judaism. When Jesus presented his message of love and compassion to the non-religious and to all other non-Jewish nations of the world, he was resisted, ridiculed, and ultimately rejected.

It's as we said in the beginning. Deadly narratives are spoken in the Christian, Muslim, and Jewish arenas that continue to stir up the deepest fears within the best people. <u>The only answer is to separate Jesus from any Western Christian cultural box and turn him loose. Jesus, simply Jesus, Jesus plus nothing, is the only one who can bring a spirit of reconciliation to these deadly, divisive narratives</u>!

JESUS BREAKS UP HOLY HUDDLES

When I began to look at Jesus with a new perspective, I discovered that he made a habit of reaching out to people from all kinds of religious and cultural backgrounds. He was inclusive, not exclusive as is so often taught. My vocational, religious blinders kept me from seeing this all-inclusive Jesus in action.

Let's examine seven encounters Jesus had with people from other nations. These are great illustrations of how he was about breaking up holy huddles and reaching out to all cultures. <u>Jesus will work with anyone and everyone</u>!

The Woman at the Well. *(John 4)* On his way from Jerusalem to Galilee, Jesus took a shortcut through Samaria. This was not the usual route Jews would take, because they were locked up in major tension with the Samaritans. The Jews strongly rejected the Samaritans and kept separate from them.

The reason? Samaritans were a mixed race and not as pure as the Jews were. The animosity between the two was intense. No trust . . . no association . . . not even conversation.

While traveling through Samaria, Jesus and his disciples stopped at the well at the town of Sychar. Jesus decided to rest at the well, but his disciples went into town to shop for food. It was noon, in the heat of the day, and a woman showed up to draw water. Jesus initiated a conversation with her. He asked for a drink. She was shocked that he, a Jew, would even speak to her. In the course of the conversation, he turns her attention to a special kind of water – living water. He explains that living water is different from well water. Sure, well water quenches physical thirst, but living water quenches the thirst of the soul. He tells her that this living water is so satisfying that she will never thirst again. In fact, this living water becomes a whole well of water within that springs up to eternal life. Naturally, she wants this kind of water. Who wouldn't?

Then Jesus gets personal. He tells her to go get her husband. She says, **"I have no husband."** Jesus replies, **"You are right. You've had five husbands and are working on the sixth!"** With this incredible insight into her life, the woman believes Jesus must be some kind of prophet. So she turns the discussion toward religion and their differences in worship. Jesus' response is unique: **"Woman, believe me, a time is coming when you will not worship God in your Samaritan way nor in the Jewish way. Soon true worshipers of God will worship in spirit and in truth, not in a certain building or location. God is looking for people to seek Him this way, since God is Spirit and Truth."**

The woman expresses that she knows God will be sending his Messiah and he will explain all things. That is when Jesus makes a shocking, some would say scandalous, declaration: **"I am he."** At that moment, the disciples show up to see their Jewish leader alone with a Samaritan woman. She quickly leaves for town to share this strange, yet wonderful, encounter she had. She tells her neighbors, **"Come see a man who told me everything I ever did! Could this be the Messiah?"** The townspeople come to the well to see Jesus for themselves. They urge him to stay with them, and he stays with them for two days. Many others believe, the text says, based on what he shares with them.

Note what happened here. Jesus shifted the discussion of well water to living water. He was interested in her and her life. Jesus already knew her and accepted her anyway. That blew her mind! Jesus wanted to show her how to be truly satisfied in a new way. He didn't argue religious or cultural differences. He pointed her to true worship of God in the heart. Jesus was not promoting any religious system. He didn't make any move to convert her to another religious system. He was offering a personal relationship with God, not an opportunity to change huddles.

The Woman from Syrophoenicia. *(Mark 7; Matthew 15)* Exhausted by the many arguments with the religious leaders, Jesus left the area for a getaway into the region of Tyre and Sidon. This is a non-Jewish area. In the home where Jesus was to stay he encountered a non-Jewish woman. Mark calls her Syrophoenician and Matthew refers to her as Canaanite. Neither was friendly to the Jews.

The Syrophoenicians or Canaanites worshiped a variety of nature gods. El was the chief god who was portrayed as a bully, and this image kept people in fear. This woman with this religious background boldly asked Jesus for help. Her daughter was tormented by evil spirits. Since her gods hadn't helped, the mother now turns to Jesus. He initially dismisses her request, but her persistence wins out.

Jesus says to her, ***"You have great faith! Your request is granted."*** Her daughter is healed that very hour. Note what happened here! Jesus honored her faith. He didn't pull her into a new religious system, didn't invite her to join a study class, didn't urge her to renounce her cultural upbringing, didn't warn her of the many man-made myths and gods of her religion.

Here's the point. This woman sought and received, and now she has her daughter whole. As a result, she went away with a special relationship with Jesus that she would never forget. Why didn't Jesus try to convert her to the one, true God and pull her away from El or polytheism – the many gods? Why didn't Jesus invite her into the "holy huddle" of Judaism? Didn't he care about keeping the holy huddle holy? Or, at least, keeping the holy huddle a huddle?

The Roman Centurion. *(Matthew 8; Luke 7)* Check out this encounter: When Jesus had entered Capernaum, a centurion came to him, asking for help. *'**Lord,**' he said, '**my servant lies at home paralyzed, suffering terribly.' Jesus said to him, 'Shall I come and heal him?' The centurion replied, 'Lord, I do not deserve to have you come under my roof. But just say the word, and my servant will be healed. For I myself am a man under authority, with soldiers under me. I tell this one, "Go," and he goes; and that one, "Come," and he comes. I say to my servant, "Do this," and he does it.'**

"When Jesus heard this, he was amazed and said to those following him, *'Truly I tell you, I have not found anyone in Israel with such great faith.'* " *(Matthew 8:6-10, NIV)*

Now, wait a minute, Jesus! This non-Jewish, Roman centurion has greater faith than you've seen in Israel? Really? But he has no religious training! How can this be? Jesus not only pronounces a non-Jew the greatest man of faith he has seen in Israel, he rubs it in deeper. Jesus goes on to say (in Matthew's version), **"Many will come to me from the east and the west, and will take their places at the feast with Abraham, Isaac and Jacob in the kingdom of heaven. But the subjects of the kingdom will be thrown outside"** *(Matthew 8:11-12, NIV).*

Those who you wouldn't think would be in God's Kingdom will be. And those you would think will surely be in the Kingdom will not be. Then Jesus says to the centurion, **"Go! Let it be done just as you believed it would"** *(Matthew 8:13, NIV).* And the centurion's servant was healed that very moment.

Note what happened here! Jesus doesn't warn the Roman centurion to avoid the many Roman gods. His concern was his faith. Jesus didn't urge this man to repent and renounce the Roman deities or his faith would not be effective.

 Why is Jesus repeatedly affirming the faith of people from other nations? Why is Jesus repeatedly exposing the lack of faith of the religious holy huddle?

The Ten Lepers. *(Luke 17)* "*Now on his way to Jerusalem, Jesus traveled along the border between Samaria and Galilee. As he was going into a village, ten men who had leprosy met him. They stood at a distance and called out in a loud voice, 'Jesus, Master, have pity on us!' When he saw them, he said, 'Go, show yourselves to the priests.' And as they went, they were cleansed. One of them, when he saw he was healed, came back, praising God in a loud voice. He threw himself at Jesus' feet and thanked him — and he was a Samaritan. Jesus asked, 'Were not all ten cleansed? Where are the other nine? Was no one found to return and give praise to*

God except this foreigner?' Then he said to him, 'Rise and go; your faith has made you well.' "
(Luke 17:11-19, NIV)

Here we go again! The star of this story is again a foreigner, a non-Jew, a Samaritan. Note we see through these stories that no matter the cultural background or religion, it's the heart that impresses Jesus the most. Here in the leper story it's a heart of gratefulness. No one from the Jewish holy huddle returned to give thanks to Jesus. Not one! Only the despised Samaritan.

The Royal Official's Son. (John 4) A royal official whose son was dying in a nearby town approached Jesus. *"**The royal official said, 'Sir, come down before my child dies.' 'Go,' Jesus replied, 'your son will live.' The man took Jesus at his word and departed. While he was still on the way, his servants met him with the news that his boy was living. When he inquired as to the time when his son got better, they said to him, 'Yesterday, at one in the afternoon, the fever left him.' Then the father realized that this was the exact time at which Jesus had said to him, 'Your son will live.' So he and his whole household believed."* (John 4:49-53, NIV).

Jesus was getting more and more upset with the religious leaders of Judaism. They followed him to Galilee from Jerusalem, after seeing the miracles he performed there. This is when the royal official asked for his own miracle. Jesus said, ***"Unless you people see signs and wonders . . . you will never believe"*** (John 4:48, NIV). In contrast to the religious leaders of Judaism, the royal official (the father) believed and the miracle followed. Again, the star of this story did not belong to the holy huddle, but was an outsider, a non-Jew, from the nations of the world who had not known God.

Feeding of the 4,000. *(Mark 8; Matthew 15)* Often when reading about Jesus' actions, you will see that he travels back and forth from one side of the Sea of Galilee to the other. Whenever they were on the Jewish side, they crossed over to the other side. Why? He performed the same works among the non-Jewish world as with the Jews. When Jesus was outside of the Jewish, holy huddle territory, he never urged them to change their religious culture, but let them remain right where they grew up. None of that seemed to matter to Jesus as long as they were drawn to him.

The Demonized Wild Man. *(Mark 5)* Again, Jesus went across the lake to the other side — to the non-Jewish side. A wild-eyed demonized man who lived in the tombs met him there. He was so filled with evil spirits that no one could bind him, not even with a chain. When his hands and feet had been chained, he broke loose. No one could control him. Night and day he cried out and cut himself with stones. Jesus commanded the evil spirits to come out of him, sending them into a herd of pigs. What a sight! He sent them into around 2,000 pigs that ran off a cliff and drowned.

Note the result of this man being freed from the demons. The wild-eyed demonized man calmed down, sitting rather than wandering around, was clothed and in his right mind. Now note the result among the people. They had been afraid of the man before, but now they were really filled with fear as they observed his miraculous transformation.

This non-Jewish, transformed man begged Jesus to let him follow along. Jesus did not let him, but said, **"Go home to your own people and tell them how much the Lord has done for you, and how he has had mercy on you"** *(Mark 5:19, NIV)*. Jesus had a mission for him to accomplish. So, the man immediately went away and began sharing his story throughout all of the Decapolis, the ten Roman cities of the region. And all the people were amazed!

All seven encounters with Jesus were with people from the nations. They were not within the Jewish holy huddle. In fact, Jesus used each of these to break up the huddle and to blow up the spirit of exclusivity that tends to rise up within such huddles. That's the spirit of the holy huddle. It's us against them. <u>Jesus is universal in his approach to the world and will have none of it</u>!

JESUS IS FOR EVERYONE

Jesus is for everyone! This makes so much sense to us, now that we know Jesus is to be lifted up above all names and came to reach out to every nation (culture) of the world.

Within the Jewish culture, Paul was often asked to speak in the local Synagogues as a guest speaker. A visiting Rabbi was always invited to share before the congregation, much like the African American Churches in this country today. BUT when Paul was in Athens, he was invited by the people in the marketplace to share his message to a non-Jewish audience. What Paul shared with this audience was brilliant! Let's check it out:

"So Paul stood in the midst of the Areopagus and said, 'Men of Athens, I observe that you are very religious in all respects. For while I was passing through and examining the objects of your worship, I also found an altar with this inscription, "TO AN UNKNOWN GOD." Therefore what you worship in ignorance, this I proclaim to you. The God who made the world and all things in it, since He is Lord of heaven and earth, does not dwell in temples made with hands; nor is He served by human hands, as though He needed anything, since <u>He Himself gives to all people life and breath and all things; and He made from one man every nation of mankind to live on all the face of the earth, having determined their appointed times and the boundaries of their habitation, that they would seek God, if perhaps they might grope for Him and find Him, though He is not far from each one of us;</u> for in Him we live and move and exist, as even some of your own poets have said, "For we also are His children." Being then the children of God, we ought not to think that the Divine Nature is like gold or silver or stone, an image formed by the art and thought of man. Therefore having overlooked the times of ignorance, God is now declaring to men that all people everywhere should repent, because He has fixed a day in which He will judge the world in righteousness through a Man whom He has appointed, having furnished proof to all men by raising Him from the dead.' " *(Acts 17:22-31, NASB)*

Note that Paul knew his audience. He stroked them for being highly religious. He didn't quote any Scripture to them, because it would have meant nothing to them. He didn't mention Jesus' name and even quoted one of their local poets, one who wrote the liturgy for the worship of Zeus.

The results were fascinating. Some began to sneer, but others said, **"We shall hear you again concerning this"** (Acts 17:32, NASB). Some also believed and joined with Paul. So, God is now declaring to men that all people everywhere need to change their minds and the direction of their lives back toward God. And, I love the words of Paul here: **"He made from one man every nation of mankind to live on all the face of the earth, having determined their appointed times and the boundaries of their habitation, that they would seek God, if perhaps they might grope for Him and find Him, though He is not far from each one of us; for in Him we live and move and exist, as even some of your own poets have said."**

 Who is Paul's audience? Why do you think some of them were interested to hear more?

 What does Paul do with respect to their religious beliefs?

How did Paul use the altar marked "TO AN UNKNOWN GOD"?

 What's the purpose of God's creative role in the world?
What does God intend for all people? Who is God reaching out to for relationship?

Possibly one of the most revolutionary scenes in the Scriptures is in Acts 10. Here is demonstrated how universal Jesus really is. Check it out!

"Now there was a man at Caesarea named Cornelius, a centurion of what was called the Italian cohort, a devout man and one who feared God with all his household, and gave many alms to the Jewish people and prayed to God continually. About the ninth hour of the day he clearly saw in a vision an angel of God who had just come in and said to him, 'Cornelius!' And fixing his gaze on him and being much alarmed, he said, 'What is it, Lord?' And he said to him, 'Your prayers and alms have ascended as a memorial before God. Now dispatch some men to Joppa and send for a man named Simon, who is also called Peter; he is staying with a tanner named Simon, whose house is by the sea.' When the angel who was speaking to him had left, he

summoned two of his servants and a devout soldier of those who were his personal attendants, and after he had explained everything to them, he sent them to Joppa." (Acts 10:1-8, NASB)

 Who was Cornelius? Was he Jewish or Christian?

 What did Cornelius do that got God's attention?

"On the next day, as they were on their way and approaching the city, Peter went up on the housetop about the sixth hour to pray. But he became hungry and was desiring to eat; but while they were making preparations, he fell into a trance; and he saw the sky opened up, and an object like a great sheet coming down, lowered by four corners to the ground, and there were in it all kinds of four-footed animals and crawling creatures of the earth and birds of the air. A voice came to him, 'Get up, Peter, kill and eat!' But Peter said, 'By no means, Lord, for I have never eaten anything unholy and unclean.' Again a voice came to him a second time, 'What God has cleansed, no longer consider unholy.' This happened three times, and immediately the object was taken up into the sky." (Acts 10:9-16, NASB)

Why did the voice from God command Peter to violate his Jewish traditions and laws? Why did this happen three times?

"Now while Peter was greatly perplexed in mind as to what the vision which he had seen might be, behold, the men who had been sent by Cornelius, having asked directions for Simon's house, appeared at the gate; and calling out, they were asking whether Simon, who was also called Peter, was staying there. While Peter was reflecting on the vision, the Spirit said to him, 'Behold, three men are looking for you. But get up, go downstairs and accompany them without misgivings, for I have sent them Myself.' Peter went down to the men and said, 'Behold, I am the one you are looking for; what is the reason for which you have come?' They said, 'Cornelius, a centurion, a righteous and God-fearing man well spoken of by the entire nation of the Jews, was divinely directed by a holy angel to send for you to come to his house and hear a message from you.' So he invited them in and gave them lodging.

"And on the next day he got up and went away with them, and some of the brethren from Joppa accompanied him. On the following day he entered Caesarea. Now Cornelius was waiting for them and had called together his relatives and close friends. When Peter entered, Cornelius met him, and fell at his feet and worshiped him. But Peter raised him up, saying, 'Stand up; I too am just a man.' As he talked with him, he entered and found many people assembled. And he said to them, 'You yourselves know how unlawful it is for a man who is a Jew to associate with a foreigner or to visit him; and yet God has shown me that I should not call any man unholy or unclean. That is why I came without even raising any objection when I was sent for. So I ask for what reason you have sent for me.'

"Cornelius said, 'Four days ago to this hour, I was praying in my house during the ninth hour; and behold, a man stood before me in shining garments, and he said, "Cornelius, your prayer has been heard and your alms have been remembered before God. Therefore send to Joppa and invite Simon, who is also called Peter, to come to you; he is staying at the house of Simon the tanner by the sea." So I sent for you immediately, and you have been kind enough to come. Now then, we are all here present before God to hear all that you have been commanded by the Lord.'

"Opening his mouth, Peter said: 'I most certainly understand now that God is not one to show partiality, but in every nation the man who fears Him and does what is right is welcome to Him.' " (Acts 10:17-35, NASB)

 What does Peter conclude about who in the world is welcomed or received by God? How does this square with what you've been taught?

Peter fought this all along the way, but then he "got it." This is exactly the word used here for understand. "Oh, now I get it!" Peter thought that if any non-Jew was going to have a chance to know God, then he must first become Jewish. Does this sound a little familiar with what you have heard within your faith communities? <u>We all think we have the way and believe others must come through our truth in order to be acceptable to God.</u> **Jesus is the way and he is universal! Jesus IS the Good News for everyone!**

JESUS IS LIFE'S FOCAL POINT!

Jesus made it clear that he was the focal point.

His revolutionary call has always been, "Follow me!" What he is saying is that the call is not to follow a religious system or a set of rules. It's "Follow me!"

It's not about following propaganda. It's not about following a program. It's about following a person. This is what sets Jesus apart from all other great leaders. He stands out by embodying his teachings. Truth is not a principle or proposition or set of beliefs. It is a person who calls all of us into relationship. Jesus didn't just teach the truth; he is the truth. He doesn't call us to simply know things, but to know him. He teaches us to be with him. Not to walk in lock-step with everything he said, without doubts or questions or confusion. But to walk alongside him, to watch and to learn. To keep company with him, to rest and to recover. To walk in rhythm with him, which is a graceful rhythm, not a forceful one. He doesn't weigh us down with the law. He lightens our load with his love. And step-by-step with him, day by day with him, we learn to live freely and lightly.

Here's how Jesus expressed it:

"Are you tired? Worn out? Burned out on religion? Come to me. Get away with me and you'll recover your life. I'll show you how to take a real rest. Walk with me and work with me – watch how I do it. Learn the unforced rhythms of grace. I won't lay anything heavy or ill-fitting on you. Keep company with me and you'll learn to live freely and lightly." (Matthew 11:28-30, MSG)

Jesus' first step in introducing this new lifestyle was to gather a small circle of men. His purpose wasn't to form a focus group to clarify his message. It wasn't to form a strategic planning committee to figure out the best way to get that message to the masses. It was to gather a few followers around him, simply to be with him *(Mark 3)*. Just him. Apparently, Jesus thought of himself as being enough to make a difference in their lives and through them to the world.

Within that circle of twelve close friends, three were the closest – Peter, James, and John. When Jesus took those three up on the mountain to pray, he was fully revealed to them, transfigured into a bright flash of lightning from head to toe. At this amazing moment, Moses and Elijah appeared in glorious splendor, talking with Jesus. When the three disciples saw this, Peter wanted to put up three shelters – one for Jesus, one for Moses, and one for Elijah. The instant he suggested it, a cloud appeared, covering them with glory and filling them with fear. A voice came from the cloud, saying, ***"This is my Son, whom I have chosen; listen to him."*** When the voice had spoken, they found that Jesus was alone. Moses, the lawgiver, and the prophet had vanished and all that was left was Jesus, simply and solely Jesus *(Luke 9)*.

JESUS ALONE IS ENOUGH?

There's a great saying that says, <u>Jesus alone is enough</u>. <u>Jesus plus anything is nothing</u>. <u>Jesus plus nothing is everything</u>. <u>And, Jesus minus nothing is just Jesus</u>.

To say that Jesus alone is enough doesn't exclude anything Jesus encompasses and brings with him. For instance, what about prayer? Well, we pray to Jesus. What about the Spirit of God mentioned in the Scriptures? The Spirit reflects, expresses, and explains Jesus as Jesus reflects, expresses, and explains God to the world. What we're actually saying by "Jesus alone is enough" is that Jesus, the name above all names, is the focal point of life — the lens by which we see everything and the filter by which we clarify all we hear and see. To say "Jesus alone is enough" or "Jesus plus nothing" means that when you follow Jesus, all that Jesus is and has comes to you. When you focus on Jesus, you have it all, because Jesus has it all! Jesus is life's focal point!

> *Think of the first of the Ten Commandments: **"You shall have no other gods before me"** (Exodus 20:3, NIV). This is the same sense and spirit of saying Jesus alone is enough. The term "before" has three meanings: No other gods (1) <u>In addition to me</u>. (2) <u>In front of me</u>. (3) <u>Instead of me</u>.*

God presented Jesus as all that anyone ever needs. When John the Baptist saw Jesus at the Jordan River, he told the crowds that he was the Lamb of God and that he is not worthy even to untie the thongs on the sandals of Jesus' feet. John believed Jesus was all you will ever need. And while John was in prison, plagued with doubts, he sent his disciples to ask Jesus, "Are you the one who was to come, or should we expect someone else?"

Jesus replied to those disciples, **"Go back and report to John what you hear and see: The blind receive sight, the lame walk, those who have leprosy are cleansed, the deaf hear, the dead are raised, and the good news is proclaimed to the poor. Blessed is anyone who does not stumble on account of me"** (Matthew 11:4-6, NIV).

John's faith was affirmed by none other than Jesus himself, assuring him that he was indeed the coming one — the focal point of John's mission and message.

After the resurrection of Jesus, his disciples were despondent and went back to fishing in the Sea of Galilee. Peter was especially feeling a sense of guilt because of his repeated denials of

Jesus back in Jerusalem. What must have been most hurtful was that Jesus warned him of his defection. Peter's response was to declare his allegiance, vowing never to do such a thing. But when he was identified that night by a small crowd around a campfire, he sweated from the fear of being handed over to the authorities, and he buckled under the peer pressure.

That would seem the end of Peter's story, but it wasn't. You would think his failure as a follower would have been grounds for dismissal. You would think his defection would have disqualified him, but notice how Jesus handled the situation.

Peter, along with several other defectors, fled to the Sea of Galilee, hoping to find solace in the familiar lapping of the waves, or at least a distraction from their pain by going fishing. That is just where Jesus shows up, not in the synagogue but on the shore, where they were. And he made them breakfast. Can you imagine what Peter was thinking? His guilt level must have been high, expecting Jesus to confront him with, "I told you so, Peter." But he didn't do that.

As they ate breakfast together, all were quiet. I'm sure they were fearful of what Jesus might be thinking and what he was going to say. After they finished the meal, Jesus turns to Peter. Can't you sense the tension? What will he say? they must have wondered. And none more so than Peter.

"Peter, do you love me?" What a shock those words must have been. Peter was expecting a lecture on duty, perhaps, and how he failed at that duty. Failed as a follower. Failed as a friend. But Jesus doesn't talk to him about duty. Rather, he talks to him about devotion. Jesus has only one concern, and it's not about responsibility but relationship. He wanted to know Peter's heart and where it stood in relation to him. Jesus wanted to give Peter a chance to declare his relationship with him, openly and without fear. A second chance. And as if that isn't shocking enough, Jesus repeats the question, giving him another opportunity to publicly declare his devotion.

"Do you love me?" "Do you love me?"

Jesus was trying to make a point with his most devoted followers. And the point is this: He is not concerned with their screw-ups or their shortcomings; he is only concerned with their relationship with him *(John 21)*. Jesus is trying to make the same point with you and with me. Our relationship with him is most vital, he's saying. Jesus is our focal point. "I am safe, warm, and welcoming, no matter what you've done or haven't done. You can come to me, without fear," Jesus says.

JESUS: THE FOCAL POINT FOR EARLY DISCIPLES

Jesus was the focal point for his early disciples and he is the focal point for his present-day disciples, too! If you doubt what Jesus is saying implicitly through that passage, look what Jesus said about himself explicitly earlier in that gospel.

"I AM the bread of life. Whoever comes to me will never go hungry, and whoever believes in me will never be thirsty." (John 6)

"I AM the light of the world. Whoever follows me will never walk in darkness, but will have the light of life." (John 8)

"I AM the gate; whoever enters through me will be saved." (John 10)

"I AM the shepherd of the sheep." (John 10)

"I AM the way, the truth and the life." (John 14)

"I AM the resurrection and the life. Anyone who believes in me will live, even though they die; and whoever lives by believing in me will never die. Do you believe this?" (John 11)

"I AM the vine." (John 15)

When Jesus taught about the dynamic relationship he wanted with his disciples, he used the illustration of the vine and the branches. He clearly taught in this section that the relationship he wants and the only one that matters is for the disciples (the branches) to cling to and stay connected to Jesus (the vine). He even went further to say, ***"Without me you can do nothing."*** Nothing. What don't we understand about nothing? How much clearer could Jesus have said it? He is life's focal point!

Clearly in this passage, and from the other I AM passages, Jesus presents himself as life's focal point – as enough for us – as all we need.

When Jesus spent his last few hours with his disciples, he gave them some of the most important principles ever given. One of the visuals Jesus used to describe his relationship with his disciples is a vine and a branch. Jesus posed himself as the vine and his disciples as branches that are so connected to the vine that they draw their very life from this relationship. The purpose of this relationship is to bear fruit.

Check out Jesus' words:

"Remain in me, as I also remain in you. No branch can bear fruit by itself; it must remain in the vine. Neither can you bear fruit unless you remain in me. I am the vine; you are the branches. <u>If you remain in me and I in you,</u> you will bear much fruit; apart from me you can do nothing. If you do not remain in me, you are like a branch that is thrown away and withers; such branches are picked up, thrown into the fire and burned. <u>If you remain in me and my words remain in you, ask whatever you wish, and it will be done for you.</u> This is to my Father's glory, that you bear much fruit, showing yourselves to be my disciples." *(John 15:4-8, NIV)*

Jesus gives one command here — to remain in him as a branch remains in a vine. To remain in Jesus is to abide in him. This might sound like a passive thing to do, but abiding in Jesus is a very active work. It is work to keep your focus on this relationship.

 Do you see how remaining connected with Jesus as a branch clings to the vine provides great perspective on how to handle what's been going wrong in your personal life, your relationships, and how you make a difference in your world?

 How we connect with Jesus to fix what's going wrong is vital to understand.

But what is this work? Jesus had an encounter that might clarify this a bit: Jesus answered, *" 'Very truly I tell you, you are looking for me, not because you saw the signs I performed but because you ate the loaves and had your fill. Do not work for food that spoils, but for food that endures to eternal life, which the Son of Man will give you. For on him God the Father has placed his seal of approval.'*

Then they asked him, 'What must we do to do the works God requires?' Jesus answered, 'The work of God is this: to believe in the one he has sent.' " (John 6:26-29, NIV)

So what is the primary work that God wants man to do? <u>TO BELIEVE JESUS</u>. <u>TO TRUST JESUS</u>! To trust Jesus is to follow the teachings and principles of Jesus — to follow him. This is work. Have you ever tried it? This is why we instruct people to share with others: "I am doing the toughest thing I've ever tried to do. I'm trying to follow the teachings and principles of Jesus." Believe me, this is the greatest work you will ever do in your life!

FOCAL POINT FOR HIS FAMILY...

Now, from the point of view of those Jesus touched or simply encountered, it's clear that to them Jesus plus nothing else was the only focal point that mattered. At the birth of Jesus there was no doubt his mother, Mary, the astronomers from the East, and the shepherds in the fields of Bethlehem all believed this was the most special baby ever to have been born.

FOCAL POINT FOR EARLY ENCOUNTERS...

There is quite a lineup of people who came later, all believing and receiving Jesus as their focal point. John the Baptist *(Matthew 3:1-17)*. Nicodemus *(John 3:1-21)*. Joseph of Arimathaea *(Luke 23:50-53)*. The woman at the well *(John 4:3-42)*. The sinful woman with the expensive perfume *(Luke 7:36-50)*. The boy with the fish and loaves *(John 6:1-15)*. The woman caught in adultery *(John 8:1-11)*. The thief on the cross *(Luke 23:40-43)*. And the soldier at the cross *(Luke 23:47)*. To name just a few.

Here are a few others. The two men who experienced the healing touch of Jesus from a distance, the Roman Centurion's servant *(Matthew 8:5-13)* and the nobleman's daughter *(4:46-54)*. They were both convinced, even before the healings, that Jesus alone was all they needed.

Those who were tormented by evil spirits certainly knew that Jesus was the Good News point of life: The demoniac in the synagogue *(Mark 1:21-28)*, for example, and the demoniac in Gadara *(Mark 5:1-20)*.

Those who were blind and given back their sight believed Jesus was enough. The blind men in Jericho *(Matthew 20:29-34)*. The blind man in Bethsaida *(Mark 8:22-26)*. And the man born blind *(John 9:1-41)*.

All who experienced Jesus' power of raising the dead believed he was the ultimate point of life. Jairus experienced the resurrection of his daughter *(Mark 5:21-43)*. Certainly he believed that Jesus was all he needed. Lazarus would also say that Jesus was life's answer, and his sisters, Mary and Martha, would wholeheartedly agree *(John 11:1-44)*. Finally, the widow of Nain, whose only son was resurrected by Jesus, surely she believed that Jesus was worthy of being her life's focus *(Luke 7:11-17)*.

All who experienced the healing touch of Jesus believed he was totally enough. Peter's mother-in-law, for example *(Matthew 8:14-17)*. The Leper *(Matthew 8:1-4)*. The woman who had been bleeding for 12 years *(Mark 5:21-43)*. The paralytic who was lowered through the roof to see Jesus *(Mark 2:1-12)*. The lame man who waited by the pool of Bethesda *(John 5:2-15)*. The man with the withered hand who showed up at the synagogue *(Matthew 12:9-21)*. The woman whose back was so bent that she was bent over permanently *(Luke 13:10-17)*. The man with dropsy *(Luke 14:1-6)*.

Although only one expressed his gratefulness to Jesus, all ten lepers experienced the truth that Jesus' word was enough to cleanse them of their leprosy *(Luke 17:11-19)*. The Syrophoenician woman who begged for her daughter to be healed *(Luke 15:21-28)*. The lame man outside Jerusalem, healed in the name of Jesus *(Acts 3)*.

Jesus' early disciples believed Jesus was their focal point *(Matthew 9:9-13; Luke 24:13-35; Acts 9)*. To make sure the point of his life didn't get lost, Jesus reiterated it to those who had been with him. Before Jesus ascended into heaven, he presented himself to his disciples and gave them many convincing proofs that he was alive. He appeared to them over a period of forty days and spoke about the Kingdom of God *(Acts 1)*. What was most important to Jesus was that his early disciples get to know him better — to hang out with him. Jesus was again making the point that he alone is enough — knowing him and his Kingdom principles was the theme of his final 40 days.

A SPECIAL ENCOUNTER AND A SPECIAL MISSION FOR PAUL...

Paul is the first follower of the Christ who meets Jesus. It was a very dramatic encounter on the road to Damascus.

"Now Saul, still breathing threats and murder against the disciples of the Lord, went to the high priest, and asked for letters from him to the synagogues at Damascus, so that if he found any belonging to the Way, both men and women, he might bring them bound to Jerusalem. As he was traveling, it happened that he was approaching Damascus, and suddenly a light from heaven flashed around him; and he fell to the ground and heard a voice saying to him, 'Saul, Saul, why are you persecuting Me?' And he said, 'Who are You, Lord?' And He said, 'I am Jesus whom you are persecuting, but get up and enter the city, and it will be told you what you must do.' " *(Acts 9:1-6)*

This is Paul's (Saul) first encounter with Jesus. He is blinded and knocked to the ground by this flash of light. When Paul asked who this was who was doing this to him, Jesus' answer wasn't "I am Jesus Christ." Nor was it "I am the Christ or the founder of Christianity." He said simply and clearly: "I am Jesus whom you are persecuting."

 Why do you think Jesus introduced himself in this way?

Now note what instructions are given for Paul: "***Now there was a disciple at Damascus named Ananias; and the Lord said to him in a vision, 'Ananias.' And he said, 'Here I am, Lord.' And the Lord said to him, 'Get up and go to the street called Straight, and inquire at the house of Judas for a man from Tarsus named Saul, for he is praying, and he has seen in a vision a man named Ananias come in and lay his hands on him, so that he might regain his sight.' But Ananias answered, 'Lord, I have heard from many about this man, how much harm he did to Your saints at Jerusalem; and here he has authority from the chief priests to bind all who call on Your name.' But the Lord said to him, 'Go, for he is a chosen instrument of Mine, <u>to bear My name before the Gentiles and kings and the sons of Israel</u>; for I will show him how much he must suffer for My name's sake' ***" (Acts 9:10-16, NASB).

 After Jesus' personal introduction to Paul and now Jesus' specific mission for Paul to bear his name to the Gentiles, the kings, and the sons of Israel, what is it that is so important about the name of Jesus? What do you think it means "to bear My name"?

Not only did Jesus make this point; his disciples were examples of this point. After Peter healed a lame man, the religious leaders confronted him and John, warning them to stop this talk about Jesus. But when they saw the courage of Peter and John, realizing that they were unschooled, ordinary men, they were astonished. And they took note that these men had been with Jesus *(Acts 4)*. The religious leaders didn't see the organizational affiliation of these men. They saw their relational affiliation. The leaders saw something in these disciples that was just Jesus. They saw that the Jesus who had been with them now lived in them and through them. Where did the disciples get that life? From being connected to the vine. All the love and forgiveness and life that flowed through that vine into them flowed through them to give life to others.

FOCAL POINT FOR PAUL & TIMOTHY...

Paul and Timothy wrote about their relationship with Jesus, too. After listing all of his educational, religious, and moral accomplishments, Paul says, **"But whatever were gains to me I now consider loss for the sake of Christ. What is more, I consider everything a loss because of the surpassing worth of knowing Christ Jesus my Lord, for whose sake I have lost all things. I consider them garbage** [manure or dung] **that I may gain Christ"** *(Philippians 3:7-8, NIV)*.

In another letter written to the Corinthians by Paul and Sosthenes, they say,

"But I am afraid that, as the serpent deceived Eve by his craftiness, your minds will be led astray from the simplicity and purity of devotion to Christ." *(2 Corinthians 11:3, NASB)*

It's about relationship, not religion, Paul is saying. It's about devotion, not doctrine. Affiliation with him, not with an organization. Jesus and all he brings to his personal encounters is enough. It's that simple – that pure and that simple.

If Jesus presented himself as life's focal point, and those he touched enthusiastically believed, why do we miss this point, which is the very essence of the Good News of Jesus?

We are able to develop entire belief systems around Jesus, enlist the masses to join our organizations around Jesus, judge those who do not quite see eye-to-eye with about Jesus, and propagate these belief systems, organizations, and dogma as the only way to life, yet all without getting to know this Jesus personally.

HOW WE EASILY MISS THE POINT

How is it that we can miss that Jesus is life's pivotal point? There are three subtle ways this occurs, in our opinion.

First, there is a tendency to add something unnecessary to Jesus. This "something" takes the form of man-made commandments and long-standing traditions; in other words, Jesus with additives *(Mark 7)*.

Second, there is a tendency to hold something sacred that has become a substitute for Jesus. These substitutes can be your sacred scriptures, your revered saints, your religious services, your particular organization or denomination, your cultural identification or religious icons.

Third, there is a tendency to leave Jesus behind. Whether it is in newsletters, religious services, sermons, articles, prayers, or worship experiences, Jesus is embarrassingly left behind! Even where two are three are gathered together in his name, he is so often left out of our conversations.

These tendencies take away from the message of Jesus. They diminish Jesus by adding something unnecessary to him, by replacing him with something, and by leaving him and his message behind. These tendencies amount to a deadly triad that keeps us from seeing Jesus clearly.

If we can't see him, how will we ever be able to know him? And if we can't know him, how will we ever be able to know if he is enough to be life's focal point?

So far, you've taken a look at Jesus — what he said and what he did. You've taken a look at what others thought about him and said about him. You've come and you've seen Jesus.

 Where are you in your thinking?

 Where do you most easily miss Jesus being your focal point?

THE END GAME IS TO CHANGE YOU & YOUR WORLD!

"The only constant in life is change."

Things are always changing! Socrates wisely said, ***"The secret of change is to focus all your energy not on fighting the old, but building the new."*** Change can be positive and life giving; change can be negative and life draining. CHOICE is the pivotal switch between the negative and the positive that determines the outcome — the end game of your life. There is another factor here. You can choose not to make a choice, but since changes are always occurring, not choosing places you in a negative mode. Things left to themselves tend to degenerate into a more disordered condition. This is where most people live. They are stuck with their feet firmly planted in mid-air, going nowhere fast!

So, you have three options regarding life-change: (1) Choose positive life-change. (2) Choose negative life-change. (3) Choose nothing and remain stuck, which produces negative life-change.

In this study session we want to focus on what produces positive life-change for you, for your relationships, and for the world around you. There are several terms we want to use in order to better understand and grasp life-change. You'll see them as we move through this study, and all revolve around Jesus.

The first life-change term is **revolution,** or being a revolutionary. We see Jesus as the most effective revolutionary. His teachings are radical and revolutionary and Jesus is the embodiment of his teachings. Jesus, the revolutionary, is a transformer who has the power to put things back together . . . better! He is the one we've found who can make things right, after we get a grip on what went wrong.

Jesus was a revolutionary in the sense that he introduced new ideas, new thoughts, and new ways of doing things, and he upset the establishment. He was a spiritual revolutionary. Let's take a thesaurus or dictionary and unpack what it means to be a revolutionary. <u>A revolutionary is radical</u> in that he takes you to the roots – the bottom line – back to the foundational core of ideas and thinking. A revolutionary is groundbreaking – an activist – sometimes world shattering. A revolutionary is innovative, progressive, sometimes rebellious, new, and different.

The second life-change term is **transformation**. Don't confuse reformation with transformation. Reform or reformation is changing something from the outside – to externally look and sound good. Reformation is never able to go far enough to bring about genuine life-change. Reformation is a little like rearranging the deck chairs on the Titanic. Transformation is to change something from the inside out. A genuine encounter with Jesus is all about transformation and not only about reformation. Jesus teaches that genuine transformation will naturally produce the necessary reforms!

 What reforms have you made in your life? Have these reforms produced any genuine transformation?

The third life-change term is **change agent**. What does it mean to be a "change agent"? A change agent is one who has experienced the transformation of God in his heart and becomes a living, personal agent of Jesus. A change agent of Jesus touches others in a variety of ways – advancing the conversation of Jesus, walking, talking, loving, and re-presenting the Good News of Jesus and the Kingdom wherever the open door presents itself. A change agent IS Jesus to others! Only God can transform a person's heart and mind. When Jesus asked his disciples, " *'But who do you say that I am?' Simon Peter answered, 'You are the Christ, the Son of the living God.' And Jesus said to him, 'Blessed are you, Simon Barjona, because flesh and blood did not reveal this to you, but My Father who is in heaven' "* (Matthew 16:15-17, NASB).

Note that Peter's answer is amazing! He says, *"You are the Christ, the Son of the living God."* Jesus quickly responded positively: *"Blessed are you, Simon."* But Jesus just as quickly points out (and this is enormous in its importance), *"Flesh and blood did not reveal this to you, but My Father who is in heaven."* This is precisely where Jesus gives us the key to how anyone experiences transformational life-change. God reveals it, himself! No human – no flesh and blood – can reveal this. No human can convince you. No human can convert you. No human can transform you.

Understanding these terms of life-change is essential to proceed toward our end game in THE WAY. Personal and people life-change is the most effective way to make a difference in our world today!

 Is making a difference in your world high on your list?

JESUS IS THE ULTIMATE CHANGE AGENT

Jesus was all of these and more! This is precisely why he was a threat to the establishment. The establishment had everything figured out, packaged neatly, and was comfortable with its thinking and its traditions. Anything new or different could be a threat.

In the fifth chapter of the gospel of Luke, Jesus did and said several things that immediately moved him into the category of a revolutionary who brought the Good News (the Gospel) to all he encountered. The radical dynamic of Jesus is more than what he teaches. <u>Jesus embodies his teachings; he is the Gospel</u>.

FIVE LIFE-CHANGING ENCOUNTERS

Let's briefly check out five Good News encounters here. **FIRST:** While Jesus was teaching on the shore of the Sea of Galilee, the crowds were growing so large that he actually climbed into a fishing boat to continue his teaching from that vantage point. Now that wasn't revolutionary. It was just a smart thing to do. When his teaching was over, he observed the fishermen washing their nets after fishing all night without a catch. Jesus urged them to take the boat out into the deep water and cast their nets. They complained that they knew their business and there were no fish out there all night long. He persisted; these seasoned fishermen cast their nets and caught more than a boatload of fish, needing help from the others to haul them in. <u>This new rabbi who had recently come on the scene proved that he was better at their profession than they were</u>. What a shocker!

✎ Is it possible that Jesus might know something about your profession? How might this be helpful (or important) for you?

✎ Are you stuck in your life right now in a place where you might ask Jesus to show you how to come out of it?

✎ Are you willing to turn your profession over to Jesus as they did?

SECOND: While he had their full attention, Jesus told them that catching fish was nothing compared to what he could see for them – <u>to become fishers of men</u>. Jesus reached out to a group of young boys who were uneducated and untrained in religious matters – a family of fishermen – and they left everything in order to follow Jesus. This was unheard of! <u>No rabbi would choose a group of men such as these common workers with the idea of making a difference in the world</u>. Jesus was picking his revolutionary team from a group of teenagers – from the junior varsity – to change the world. Can you relate to the idea that Jesus would work with those people who might not be "first choice" in our culture's way of thinking?

 Is there anything that Jesus seems to be telling you to do other than what you are doing now?

 What would you think of being part of a group of people who met together regularly to do something that makes a difference?

THIRD: In a nearby city in the Galilee area a leper approached Jesus, seeking healing from him. A leper is a person who is avoided or rejected by others for moral, social, and religious reasons. Lepers represent the "untouchables" in our world. Leprosy is a chronic infection of the skin, usually without symptoms and typically remains this way from five to twenty years. This may result in a lack of ability to feel pain and therefore the loss of parts of extremities due to repeated injuries or infections due to unnoticed wounds. Jesus didn't walk away as was the custom and required by the law. Jesus reached out and touched the untouchable leper! Through this daring and powerful move, the leper was miraculously healed and became a clean man as a result. Now that was revolutionary good news to the leper!

✎ What does this encounter say about Jesus and his Kingdom? Can you identify with Jesus touching an "untouchable" person?

✎ Do you believe Jesus can touch your untouchable things, things that only you and Jesus know about?

✎ What are the untouchable things you have in your community?

✎ Is there any good reason why Jesus couldn't do this same kind of miracle today? Can you see yourself seeking after Jesus to do the same or a similar thing in your life?

FOURTH: A paralytic was brought to Jesus so that he might heal him. His friends went to so much trouble to get their crippled friend in front of Jesus by lowering him through the roof of the house where Jesus was teaching. It was obvious what the need was and why the paralytic was brought to Jesus. He needed physical healing. But instead of healing his paralysis – his physical problem – Jesus went deeper into his soul and forgave him of his sins – his spiritual problem. Talk about an act of revolution! Jesus knew very well the new and different approach he had taken and he said, *" 'Which is easier, to say, "Your sins have been forgiven you," or to say, "Get up and walk"? But, so that you may know that the Son of Man has authority on earth to forgive sins' – He said to the paralytic, 'I say to you, get up, and pick up your stretcher and go home.' Immediately he got up before them, and picked up what he had been lying on, and went home glorifying God. They were all struck with astonishment and began glorifying God; and they were filled with fear, saying, 'We have seen remarkable things today' "* (Luke 5:23-26, NASB).

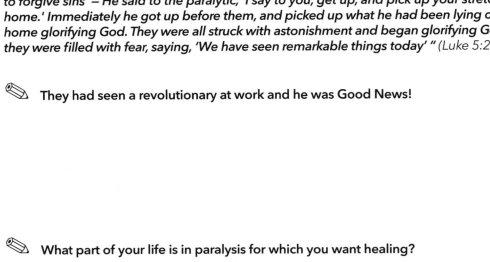

✏️ **They had seen a revolutionary at work and he was Good News!**

✏️ **What part of your life is in paralysis for which you want healing?**

✏️ **Why is it easier to say, "Your sins have been forgiven you" than to say, "Get up and walk"?**

FIFTH: Jesus, the new rabbi (teacher) in town, approached the hated tax collector, Matthew, and made an offer to him. Jesus said, ***"Follow me."*** These very words spoke complete acceptance of Matthew as being approved and good enough to follow the new rabbi, which was the goal of most young Jewish students. <u>Matthew had never been viewed by any rabbi as acceptable and good enough, until now</u>. Matthew was so thrilled that he threw a party with all of his "sinner," non-religious friends.

 Why do you think Matthew so quickly responded to Jesus by following him?

 What does it take for you to respond to Jesus' calling to follow him?

 Do you think of yourself as not worthy of doing anything good?

These were all revolutionary and life-changing actions by Jesus, and now Jesus introduces a vivid image of how he viewed his revolutionary teachings. When Jesus is questioned about his unorthodox actions and non-traditional practices, he uses a fascinating image to explain himself and his thinking that motivates how he lives.

The Pharisees and their scribes began grumbling at his disciples. In response, Jesus says, " 'It *is not those who are well who need a physician, but those who are sick. I have not come to call the righteous but sinners to repentance. . . . And He was also telling them a parable: 'No one tears a piece of cloth from a new garment and puts it on an old garment; otherwise he will both tear the new, and the piece from the new will not match the old. And no one puts new wine into old wineskins; otherwise the new wine will burst the skins and it will be spilled out, and the skins will be ruined. But new wine must be put into fresh wineskins' "* (Luke 5:31-32,36-38, NASB).

Jesus, the revolutionary, envisions his teachings and movement of followers as "new wine" and all other traditional establishment forms as "old wineskins." He warns that the new wine — his new way of thinking and even his new followers — will, by their very nature, be unable to contain the new wine. In other words, Jesus' "new wine" movement is so new and different — so revolutionary — that the traditional, man-made structures cannot contain the movement. The Jesus revolution is going on right now close to where you live. The revolution of Jesus, the revolutionary, is still on today and Jesus is the best news ever!

Paul's words in his second letter to the Corinthians continue to haunt: *"I am afraid that as the serpent deceived Eve by his craftiness, your minds will be led astray from the simplicity and purity of devotion to Christ"* (2 Corinthians 11: 3, NASB). We want to be in the spirit of simplicity and purity and share with you JESUS . . . JUST JESUS.

What is it that Jesus can give you that you can't get on your own? This may sound a bit strange, but Jesus came as a revolutionary. The revolution is all about the Good News of restoration and transformation. Jesus, the revolutionary, is the Good News — life-changing news!

LIFE-CHANGE STARTS WITH <u>YOU,</u> <u>THEN</u> TO YOUR WORLD!

For life-change to be comprehensive and most pervasive, the transformation must resonate from the inside out. When genuine transformation occurs in the heart of a person, nothing can stop the viral spread of the effects of the life-change.

Three life-changing Jesus encounters immediately come to mind that illustrate how personal life-change naturally radiates to others. We've briefly viewed two of these Jesus encounters and the other three are even more powerful. Let's examine each one to better understand how important it is that global transformation is the natural outflow of personal transformation. It's as basic as Mahatma Gandhi's life observation: Be the change you want to see in the world.

FIRST: The Samaritan woman. *(John 4)* This is a very familiar story of Jesus' encounter with a Samaritan woman at the well in the middle of the day. It was an unlikely encounter for a Jewish man and a Samaritan woman to meet together under any circumstances. After a fascinating conversation about the well water that the woman could provide compared to the living water that only Jesus could provide, Jesus says, *" 'Everyone who drinks of this water will thirst again; but whoever drinks of the water that I will give him shall never thirst; but the water that I will give him will become in him a well of water springing up to eternal life.' The woman said to Him, 'Sir, give me this water, so I will not be thirsty nor come all the way here to draw.' He said to her, 'Go, call your husband and come here.' The woman answered and said, 'I have no husband.' Jesus said to her, 'You have correctly said, "I have no husband"; for you have had five husbands, and the one whom you now have is not your husband; this you have said truly.' The woman said to Him, 'Sir, I perceive that You are a prophet.' . . .*

" 'An hour is coming, and now is, when the true worshipers will worship the Father in spirit and truth; for such people the Father seeks to be His worshipers. God is spirit, and those who worship Him must worship in spirit and truth.'

"The woman said to Him, 'I know that Messiah is coming (He who is called the Christ); when that One comes, He will declare all things to us.' Jesus said to her, 'I who speak to you am He.'

"At this point His disciples came, and they were amazed that He had been speaking with a woman, yet no one said, 'What do You seek?' or, 'Why do You speak with her?' "
(John 4:13-19,23-27, NASB)

 What happened to the woman in her encounter with Jesus that changed her thinking?

 What strikes you about Jesus here?

From that pivotal life-changing conversation with Jesus, she reached out to the leaders of her city.

"So the woman left her waterpot, and went into the city and said to the men, 'Come, see a man who told me all the things that I have done; this is not the Christ, is it?' They went out of the city, and were coming to Him." (John 4:28-30, NASB)

 What did she share with the city leaders that caused them to come out of the city to see Jesus?

"From that city many of the Samaritans believed in Him because of the word of the woman who testified, 'He told me all the things that I have done.' So when the Samaritans came to Jesus, they were asking Him to stay with them; and He stayed there two days. Many more believed because of His word; and they were saying to the woman, 'It is no longer because of what you said that we believe, for we have heard for ourselves and know that this One is indeed the Savior of the world.' " (John 4:39-42, NASB)

 What was the result of the woman's life-changing conversation with Jesus for the people of her city?

Can you see yourself advancing the conversation of Jesus with others, pointing them to see Jesus for themselves?

 Can you imagine who these "others" might be in your life?

SECOND: Matthew, The Tax Collector. *(Matthew 9)* In Jesus' calling of Matthew to follow him, Matthew somehow sensed the love and acceptance of this new Rabbi Jesus and responded to his call. This encounter is not so dramatic or showy, such as a healing. This encounter was only evidenced by Matthew, apparently, leaving his vocational post of collecting taxes. **"As Jesus went on from there, He saw a man called Matthew, sitting in the tax collector's booth; and He said to him, 'Follow Me!' And he got up and followed Him"** *(Matthew 9:9, NASB).*

There was something in this encounter between Jesus and Matthew that was indeed life changing. Matthew shifted his position in the community. He was once known as a non-spiritual businessman, who was not well liked because of his position of being the local tax collector. Then, he leaves that "standing" in the community and commits to follow in the footsteps of the new Rabbi Jesus. And, he did this with no religious training whatsoever! Now look at the result of his life-changing experience and decision to follow Jesus: *"**Then it happened that as Jesus was reclining at the table in the house, behold, many tax collectors and sinners came and were dining with Jesus and His disciples. When the Pharisees saw this, they said to His disciples, 'Why is your Teacher eating with the tax collectors and sinners?' But when Jesus heard this, He said, 'It is not those who are healthy who need a physician, but those who are sick. But go and learn what this means: "I desire compassion, and not sacrifice," for I did not come to call the righteous, but sinners,'** (Matthew 9:10-13, NASB).*

How would you describe the results of Matthew's life-changing encounter with Jesus? How might others experience this same kind of transformation?

What are the possibilities of you or others experiencing this same kind of transformation?

What is it that may be most attractive about Matthew's story? What makes his story most compelling?

What about your story? Are you afraid of other people or some things in your story that hinder you to follow Jesus?

THIRD: The Changed Demoniac. *(Mark 5)* In this third life-changing encounter with Jesus, we see a wild man who was known throughout the area as the man who wandered among the graves with blood-curdling screams. This man was crazy and out of control. Chains couldn't even hold him down. Then, Jesus encountered him! This promised to be a dramatic encounter!

"They came to the other side of the sea, into the country of the Gerasenes. When He got out of the boat, immediately a man from the tombs with an unclean spirit met Him, and he had his dwelling among the tombs. And no one was able to bind him anymore, even with a chain; because he had often been bound with shackles and chains, and the chains had been torn apart by him and the shackles broken in pieces, and no one was strong enough to subdue him. Constantly, night and day, he was screaming among the tombs and in the mountains, and gashing himself with stones. Seeing Jesus from a distance, he ran up and bowed down before Him; and shouting with a loud voice, he said, 'What business do we have with each other, Jesus, Son of the Most High God? I implore You by God, do not torment me!' For He had been saying to him, 'Come out of the man, you unclean spirit!' And He was asking him, 'What is your name?' And he said to Him, 'My name is Legion; for we are many.' And he began to implore Him earnestly not to send them out of the country. Now there was a large herd of swine feeding nearby on the mountain. The demons implored Him, saying, 'Send us into the swine so that we may enter them.' Jesus gave them permission. And coming out, the unclean spirits entered the swine; and the herd rushed down the steep bank into the sea, about two thousand of them; and they were drowned in the sea.

"Their herdsmen ran away and reported it in the city and in the country. And the people came to see what it was that had happened. They came to Jesus and observed the man who had been demonized sitting down, clothed and in his right mind, the very man who had had the 'legion'; and they became frightened." (Mark 5:1-15, NASB)

   What life-change did the demoniac experience?

   The people were afraid of the demoniac before his encounter with Jesus, so why are they now afraid again?

Are there crazy things in your life that need to be changed?

The people of the village who witnessed this dramatic healing were touched by the transformation of the demoniac. But there's more! Listen to the response of the demoniac to Jesus and his request of Jesus. "*As He [Jesus] was getting into the boat, the man who had been demon-possessed was imploring Him that he might accompany Him. And He did not let him, but He said to him, 'Go home to your people and report to them what great things the Lord has done for you, and how He had mercy on you.' And he went away and began to proclaim in Decapolis what great things Jesus had done for him; and everyone was amazed"* (Mark 5:18-20, NASB).

 What did the demoniac ask of Jesus? Why do you think the demoniac wanted to follow along with Jesus and his other disciples?

 What was Jesus' response to him? What do you think the purpose was for sending him back to his own people?

Who are your "own" people? Do you go back and tell your people what Jesus did to you?

WHAT IS INVOLVED IN THE PROCESS OF TRANSFORMATION?

There is the story of the healing of the man who was born blind. It's the most extensive miracle story in the Scriptures . . . and one of the most humorous. Let's examine the process of how the blind man was not only made to see physically, but able to see Jesus spiritually. Note the four stages of growth in the blind man's understanding of Jesus. *"As He passed by, He saw a man blind from birth. And His disciples asked Him, 'Rabbi, who sinned, this man or his parents, that he would be born blind?' Jesus answered, 'It was neither that this man sinned, nor his parents; but it was so that the works of God might be displayed in him. We must work the works of Him who sent Me as long as it is day; night is coming when no one can work. While I am in the world, I am the Light of the world.' When He had said this, He spat on the ground, and made clay of the spittle, and applied the clay to his eyes, and said to him, 'Go, wash in the pool of Siloam' (which is translated, Sent). So he went away and washed, and came back seeing. Therefore the neighbors, and those who previously saw him as a beggar, were saying, 'Is not this the one who used to sit and beg?' Others were saying, 'This is he,' still others were saying, 'No, but he is like him.' He kept saying, 'I am the one.' So they were saying to him, 'How then were your eyes opened?' He answered, 'The man who is called Jesus made clay, and anointed my eyes, and said to me, "Go to Siloam and wash"; so I went away and washed, and I received sight.' They said to him, 'Where is He?' He said, 'I do not know.'* [#1]

"They brought to the Pharisees the man who was formerly blind. Now it was a Sabbath on the day when Jesus made the clay and opened his eyes. Then the Pharisees also were asking him again how he received his sight. And he said to them, 'He applied clay to my eyes, and I washed, and I see.' Therefore some of the Pharisees were saying, 'This man is not from God, because He does not keep the Sabbath.' But others were saying, 'How can a man who is a sinner perform such signs?' And there was a division among them. So they said to the blind man again, 'What do you say about Him, since He opened your eyes?' And he said, 'He is a prophet.' [#2]

"The Jews then did not believe it of him, that he had been blind and had received sight, until they called the parents of the very one who had received his sight, and questioned them, saying, 'Is this your son, who you say was born blind? Then how does he now see?' His parents answered them and said, 'We know that this is our son, and that he was born blind; but how he now sees, we do not know; or who opened his eyes, we do not know. Ask him; he is of age, he will speak for himself.' His parents said this because they were afraid of the Jews; for the Jews had already agreed that if anyone confessed Him to be Christ, he was to be put out of the synagogue. For this reason his parents said, 'He is of age; ask him.'

"So a second time they called the man who had been blind, and said to him, 'Give glory to God; we know that this man is a sinner.' He then answered, 'Whether He is a sinner, I do not know; one thing I do know, that though I was blind, now I see.' So they said to him, 'What did He do to you? How did He open your eyes?' He answered them, 'I told you already and you did not listen; why do you want to hear it again? You do not want to become His disciples too, do you?' They reviled him and said, 'You are His disciple, but we are disciples of Moses. We know that God has spoken to Moses, but as for this man, we do not know where He is from.' The man answered and said to them, 'Well, here is an amazing thing, that you do not know where He is from, and yet He opened my eyes. <u>We know that God does not hear sinners; but if anyone is God-fearing and does His will, He hears him.</u> Since the beginning of time it has never been heard that anyone opened the eyes of a person born blind. If this man were not from God, He could do nothing.' [#3] They answered him, 'You were born entirely in sins, and are you teaching us?' So they put him out.

"Jesus heard that they had put him out, and finding him, He said, 'Do you believe in the Son of Man?' He answered, 'Who is He, Lord, that I may believe in Him?' Jesus said to him, 'You have both seen Him, and He is the one who is talking with you.' And he said, <u>'Lord, I believe.' And he worshiped Him.</u> [#4] And Jesus said, 'For judgment I came into this world, so that those who do not see may see, and that those who see may become blind.' Those of the Pharisees who were with Him heard these things and said to Him, 'We are not blind too, are we?' Jesus said to them, 'If you were blind, you would have no sin; but since you say, "We see," your sin remains.' "
(John 9:1-41, NASB)

It's interesting to watch the progression of faith in this once-blind man. He moves from one who hardly knows of Jesus to a worshipper of Jesus. His first view of Jesus was **"the man called Jesus"** who opened his blind eyes. Then, when questioned, he reasoned, **"He must be a prophet."** His next logical reasoning was, **"We know that God does not hear sinners; but if anyone is God-fearing and does His will, He hears him."** Therefore, this man called Jesus is somehow connected with God. Then, after the formerly blind man was thrown out of the Temple, Jesus goes to him and elicits this response from him: **" 'Lord, I believe.' And he worshiped Him."** <u>Not only can the man born blind see physically, he now sees spiritually and is moved to believe in the man Jesus who opened his eyes</u>!

At which stage are you in your relationship with Jesus?

HOW TO BECOME A CHANGE AGENT

In Acts 3 Peter and John were involved in an astounding healing of a crippled man. Check it out:
"Now Peter and John were going up to the temple at the ninth hour, the hour of prayer. And a man who had been lame from his mother's womb was being carried along, whom they used to set down every day at the gate of the temple, which is called Beautiful, in order to beg alms of those who were entering the temple. When he saw Peter and John about to go into the temple, he began asking to receive alms. But Peter, along with John, fixed his gaze on him and said, 'Look at us!' And he began to give them his attention, expecting to receive something from them. But Peter said, 'I do not possess silver and gold, but what I do have I give to you: In the name of Jesus Christ the Nazarene – walk!' And seizing him by the right hand, he raised him up; and immediately his feet and his ankles were strengthened. With a leap he stood upright and began to walk; and he entered the temple with them, walking and leaping and praising God. And all the people saw him walking and praising God; and they were taking note of him as being the one who used to sit at the Beautiful Gate of the temple to beg alms, and they were filled with wonder and amazement at what had happened to him.

"While he was clinging to Peter and John, all the people ran together to them at the so-called portico of Solomon, full of amazement." (Acts 3:1-11, NASB)

 What is the life changing experience here for the lame man? For Peter and John?

What was the surprise for the lame man?

 What is the surprise for you in finding Jesus? Were you crippled in your family, in your job, in your relationships, in your dreams?

This life-changing encounter is different from what we've seen. Jesus encountered a person who was crippled since birth through his followers. The life-change above not only occurred in the person in need; it also occurred in the change agents Jesus used to deliver the transformation. The problem with being a change agent for Jesus is that people will do everything they can to discount you or what you're doing and to even control what Jesus is doing through you.

"On the next day, their rulers and elders and scribes were gathered together in Jerusalem; and Annas the high priest was there, and Caiaphas and John and Alexander, and all who were of high-priestly descent. When they had placed them in the center, they began to inquire, 'By what power, or in what name, have you done this?' Then Peter, filled with the Holy Spirit, said to them, 'Rulers and elders of the people, if we are on trial today for a benefit done to a sick man, as to how this man has been made well, let it be known to all of you and to all the people of Israel, that by the name of Jesus Christ the Nazarene, whom you crucified, whom God raised from the dead — by this name this man stands here before you in good health.' "
(Acts 4:5-10, NASB)

In the next part of the story, we see who Jesus was looking for to use as change agents. **NOTE** who Jesus chose as change agents:

"Now <u>as they observed the confidence of Peter and John and understood that they were uneducated and untrained men, they were amazed, and began to recognize them as having been with Jesus. And seeing the man who had been healed, standing with them, they had nothing to say in reply."</u> (Acts 4:13-15, NASB)

What are the qualifications for being change agents for Jesus?

1.

2.

3.

4.

"But when they had ordered them to leave the Council, they began to confer with one another, saying, 'What shall we do with these men? For the fact that a noteworthy miracle has taken place through them is apparent to all who live in Jerusalem, and we cannot deny it. But so that it will not spread any further among the people, let us warn them to speak no longer to any man in this name.' And when they had summoned them, they commanded them not to speak or teach at all in the name of Jesus. But Peter and John answered and said to them, 'Whether it is right in the sight of God to give heed to you rather than to God, you be the judge; for we cannot stop speaking about what we have seen and heard.' " (Acts 4:15-20, NASB)

NOTE the change agents could not be stopped. Once you know the transformation of Jesus in your life, you will learn to become a stubborn follower of Jesus who *"cannot stop speaking about what [you've] seen and heard."*

 Are you ready to be a change agent for Jesus?

HOW TO EXPERIENCE THE PRESENCE OF JESUS!

Jesus made an astounding statement about what his followers will be able to do:

"Truly, truly, I say to you, he who believes in Me, the works that I do, he will do also; and greater works than these he will do; because I go to the Father." (John 14:12, NASB)

 What are some other words that might mean the same as "believes in me"?

NOTE what Jesus says those who believe in him can do. <u>You'll be able to do the works Jesus does AND you will be able to do greater works than the works of Jesus.</u> Whatever term you use — to believe, trust, follow — there is no great feat that one must do here to be able to do the works Jesus does and to even do greater works than Jesus did. Keep in mind that Jesus is speaking to his early disciples here but this is also true for all of Jesus' disciples everywhere in every generation.

 What does Jesus mean by "the works that I do"? What does Jesus mean by "greater works than these he will do"?

JESUS IS YOUR COMFORTER – YOUR HELPER

In addition to his followers being able to do the works that he did and doing greater works than what he did, Jesus intensifies what he is offering his followers with another incredible statement, almost as explosive as the first one. "***Whatever you ask in My name, that will I do***, *so that the Father may be glorified in the Son.*" *(John 14:13, NASB)*

Jesus invites his followers to ask "whatever" in his name and he will act upon it. He will act on it, so that the Father will be glorified – radiated and reflected – in the Son. Whatever you ask in his name, Jesus will focus all of his wisdom and power upon that request!

"My little children, I am writing these things to you so that you may not sin. And if anyone sins, we have an Advocate with the Father, Jesus Christ the righteous." (1 John 2:1)

NOTE that Jesus is called our advocate. Advocate is translated from the word "Paraclete," one who is called alongside to help, a friend who is a comforter. Jesus' role from the beginning with his followers was to be a friend who walked beside them along the way. So, when we refer to the habit of learning to walk with Jesus, it's so that you can seek his counsel, strength, and comfort daily. Can you imagine what it was like to walk alongside Jesus as his early disciples did as you are doing life together?

 How would that change your daily walk on your journey?

And all of this has a pre-requisite – a condition attached to it. In a sense, this condition is a context that Jesus wants with his followers. "*If you love Me, you will keep My commandments*" *(John 14:15, NASB).*

 How would you restate this condition in your own words?

The condition is that Jesus wants to be in relationship with you – in sync. Being in sync implies a personal, loving relationship that desires to talk and listen to him, as well as please him. This is the essence of the friendship that Jesus wants with his followers. ***"This is My commandment, that you love one another, just as I have loved you. Greater love has no one than this, that one lay down his life for his friends. <u>You are My friends if you do what I command you. No longer do I call you slaves, for the slave does not know what his master is doing; but I have called you friends, for all things that I have heard from My Father I have made known to you</u>. You did not choose Me but I chose you, and appointed you that you would go and bear fruit, and that your fruit would remain, so that whatever you ask of the Father in My name He may give to you. This I command you, that you love one another"*** *(John 15:12-17, NASB)*.

Jesus no longer wants his followers to be viewed as slaves or even bond-slaves, as Paul states in his writings. Jesus wants his relationship with his followers to be as friends. This was a revolutionary thought to his early followers and it is also radical thinking today.

 How would you describe the difference in your own thinking between following Jesus as his slave and following Jesus as his friend? What difference does this make for you?

JESUS OFFERS "ANOTHER" COMFORTER – HELPER

Earlier we were imagining what it would have been like to have Jesus right beside us as we follow him, as the early disciples did. Well, Jesus now offers something that could blow your mind.

Jesus is about to go away from his disciples, but he is not going to leave them to be alone without his presence. He reveals to them that he will ask the Father to give them "another helper," who will be with them forever!

So, even though Jesus is leaving them, his disciples will still have the same sort of presence of Jesus with them. Now, there's a huge difference with respect to the Holy Spirit, the Helper, the Spirit of truth, from the presence of Jesus the early disciples experienced. Let's examine this new presence of Jesus.

"I will ask the Father, and He will give you another Helper, that He may be with you forever . . . The Spirit of truth . . . abides with you and will be in you." (John 14:16-17, NASB)

FIRST: <u>Jesus promises another helper, another "Paraclete," which is one who is called alongside to help.</u> This second Paraclete has the capability and adaptability for giving aid as needed. Jesus identifies this second Paraclete as "another" comforter, which means another of the same sort as Jesus and not different from Jesus. Jesus goes on to identify this Paraclete or helper as the Spirit of truth twice and then reveals him as the Holy Spirit.

SECOND: <u>This new Helper, the Holy Spirit, will be with Jesus' disciples forever</u>! The presence of Jesus can be a reality forever. Now, that's a long time. This is how Jesus could promise his disciples that he would be with them until the end of time. The presence of Jesus will continue with the followers of Jesus forever through the Spirit!

THIRD: <u>The Spirit will not only be with you; he will be in you</u>. Now, here may be the most important part of the presence of Jesus through the Spirit in the lives of his followers. The Holy Spirit will permanently indwell each genuine follower of Jesus. This means we don't need to ask the Spirit to be with us. We don't need to invite the Spirit into our lives, our meetings, and our pain. Jesus is already with us and is in us through the indwelling Holy Spirit.

This very fact of the presence of the Holy Spirit in our lives is powerfully referenced by Paul in his letter to the gathering of followers in Corinth: *"**Or do you not know that your body is a temple of the Holy Spirit who is in you, whom you have from God, and that you are not your own? For you have been bought with a price: therefore glorify God in your body"** (1 Corinthians 6:19-20, NASB):*

 What do you think Paul means by "your body is a temple of the Holy Spirit"? What is our responsibility, if we consider our bodies to be a temple – a dwelling place of God?

This is revolutionary talk and the most profound insight about how the presence of Jesus is available to all who follow in the footsteps of Jesus. The Holy Spirit, the Spirit of truth, has always been the presence of God from the beginning. Remember David's references to the Spirit? ***"Do not cast me from your presence or take your Holy Spirit from me"*** *(Psalm 51:11, NIV).* *"Where can I go from your Spirit? Where can I flee from your presence?" (Psalm 139:7, NIV).*

This same Holy Spirit is now powerfully present in you – the presence of Jesus – the presence of God.

 When you think of the Holy Spirit actually living in you right now, what does this mean to you?

THE BAPTISM OF THE HOLY SPIRIT

Just before John baptized Jesus, John was becoming more and more popular in his preaching. His message was clearly two-fold: (1) He challenged people who came to him to repent – to change the direction of their thinking and their lives before God. (2) He came preparing the way for God's promised Messiah. At one point, John distinguished himself from Jesus, when he said, **"As for me, I baptize you with water for repentance, but He who is coming after me is mightier than I, and I am not fit to remove His sandals; He will baptize you with the Holy Spirit and fire"** *(Matthew 3:11, NIV).*

The term "baptism" has to do with the act of identification. By water baptism, John identified people with this renewed Kingdom movement in anticipation of receiving and following after the Messiah. Jesus' form of baptism had to do with having a new identification through the power of the Holy Spirit, coming upon a believer in Jesus. This Spirit baptism was the powerful transition of the Spirit being with believers to the permanent indwelling of the Spirit of God within the believer.

After Jesus' resurrection, Jesus met with his early disciples one last time. **NOTE** what happens: **"To these He also presented Himself alive after His suffering, by many convincing proofs, appearing to them over a period of forty days and speaking of the things concerning the kingdom of God. Gathering them together, He commanded them not to leave Jerusalem, but to wait for what the Father had promised, 'Which,' He said, 'you heard of from Me; for John**

baptized with water, but you will be baptized with the Holy Spirit not many days from now . . .
but you will receive power when the Holy Spirit has come upon you; and you shall be My
witnesses both in Jerusalem, and in all Judea and Samaria, and even to the remotest part of the
earth' " (Acts 1:3-5; 8, NASB).

 What did Jesus command his disciples to wait for in Jerusalem?

 And, what does Jesus say the Holy Spirit will do to them?

Throughout history in Scripture, the Holy Spirit came upon believers temporarily for special messaging and for performing special tasks. NOW, Jesus introduces the baptism of the Holy Spirit, which is when the Holy Spirit comes upon a believer to indwell him permanently. This was a first. It had never happened before! <u>Believers in Jesus would at some point be permanently indwelt by the Holy Spirit</u>.

There seem to be four groups of believers who experience this baptism of the Holy Spirit. In other words, they were already believers and this new, revolutionary presence of Jesus – the Holy Spirit – came upon these groups in a powerful way. Let's look at them all.

FIRST GROUP: JERUSALEM BELIEVERS

"When the day of Pentecost had come, they were all together in one place. And suddenly there came from heaven a noise like a violent rushing wind, and it filled the whole house where they were sitting. And there appeared to them tongues as of fire distributing themselves, and they rested on each one of them. And they were all filled with the Holy Spirit and began to speak with other tongues, as the Spirit was giving them utterance.

"Now there were Jews living in Jerusalem, devout men from every nation under heaven. And when this sound occurred, the crowd came together, and were bewildered because each one of them was hearing them speak in his own language. They were amazed and astonished, saying, 'Why, are not all these who are speaking Galileans? And how is it that we each hear them in our own language to which we were born? Parthians and Medes and Elamites, and residents of Mesopotamia, Judea and Cappadocia, Pontus and Asia, Phrygia and Pamphylia, Egypt and the districts of Libya around Cyrene, and visitors from Rome, both Jews and proselytes, Cretans and Arabs – we hear them in our own tongues speaking of the mighty deeds of God.' And they all continued in amazement and great perplexity, saying to one another, 'What does this mean?' " (Acts 2:1-12, NASB)

 What happened when the Holy Spirit came upon these believers?

SECOND GROUP: SAMARITAN BELIEVERS

"Therefore, those who had been scattered went about preaching the word. Philip went down to the city of Samaria and began proclaiming Christ to them. The crowds with one accord were giving attention to what was said by Philip, as they heard and saw the signs which he was performing. For in the case of many who had unclean spirits, they were coming out of them shouting with a loud voice; and many who had been paralyzed and lame were healed. So there was much rejoicing in that city. . . .

"But when they believed Philip preaching the good news about the kingdom of God and the name of Jesus Christ, they were being baptized, men and women alike. Even Simon himself believed; and after being baptized, he continued on with Philip, and as he observed signs and great miracles taking place, he was constantly amazed.

"Now when the apostles in Jerusalem heard that Samaria had received the word of God, they sent them Peter and John, who came down and prayed for them that they might receive the Holy Spirit. For He had not yet fallen upon any of them; they had simply been baptized in the name of the Lord Jesus. Then they began laying their hands on them, and they were receiving the Holy Spirit." (Acts 8:4-8,12-17)

 What happened when the Holy Spirit came upon these believers?

THIRD GROUP: GENTILE BELIEVERS

"Cornelius, a centurion, a righteous and God-fearing man well spoken of by the entire nation of the Jews, was divinely directed by a holy angel to send for you to come to his house and hear a message from you." (Acts 10:22, NASB)

"While Peter was still speaking these words, the Holy Spirit fell upon all those who were listening to the message. All the circumcised believers who came with Peter were amazed, because the gift of the Holy Spirit had been poured out on the Gentiles also. For they were hearing them speaking with tongues and exalting God. Then Peter answered, 'Surely no one can refuse the water for these to be baptized who have received the Holy Spirit just as we did, can he?' And he ordered them to be baptized in the name of Jesus Christ. Then they asked him to stay on for a few days." (Acts 10:22, 44-48, NASB)

 What happened when the Holy Spirit came upon these believers?

FOURTH GROUP: DISCIPLES OF JOHN

"It happened that while Apollos was at Corinth, Paul passed through the upper country and came to Ephesus, and found some disciples. He said to them, 'Did you receive the Holy Spirit when you believed?' And they said to him, 'No, we have not even heard whether there is a Holy Spirit.' And he said, 'Into what then were you baptized?' And they said, 'Into John's baptism.' Paul said, 'John baptized with the baptism of repentance, telling the people to believe in Him who was coming after him, that is, in Jesus.' When they heard this, they were baptized in the name of the Lord Jesus. And when Paul had laid his hands upon them, the Holy Spirit came on them, and they began speaking with tongues and prophesying. There were in all about twelve men." (Acts 19:1-7, NASB)

 What happened when the Holy Spirit came upon these believers?

 How would you describe these four different groups of people in terms of similar people from your own culture?

After these initial groups of believers experienced the baptism of the Holy Spirit, by which the Spirit powerfully came upon them to permanently indwell them forever, what happened next? There's an interesting teaching by Paul as he addressed the followers of Jesus in the city of Corinth. *"**For by one Spirit we were all baptized into one body, whether Jews or Greeks, whether slaves or free, and we were all made to drink of one Spirit**" (1 Corinthians 12:13, NASB).*

 With that in mind, what do you think it means that "we were all baptized into one body . . . and we were all made to drink of one Spirit"?

 Could it be that all believers are automatically baptized by the Holy Spirit and now have the Holy Spirit permanently indwelling them?

WHAT DOES THE HOLY SPIRIT DO IN AND THROUGH YOU?

In essence, the full and complete work of the Holy Spirit in the life of a follower of Jesus is to enable a believer to walk, talk, think, and love like Jesus. The Spirit's primary responsibility is to be your silent partner — the very presence of Jesus in your life! The Holy Spirit will keep you on track to make Jesus the focal point in your life.

There's no way to talk here about everything the Holy Spirit does, but let's move through several of the things that a follower of Jesus would do well to keep in mind. The key to experiencing the presence of Jesus is to be aware of what his presence — the Spirit — is up to.

Let's list several activities of the Spirit as he indwells within the believer/follower of Jesus. After each listing, put your observation in your own words.

- *"He will not speak on His own initiative, but whatever He hears, He will speak; and He will disclose to you what is to come. He will glorify Me; for He shall take of Mine, and shall disclose it to you"* (John 16:13-14, NASB).

What is the Spirit doing here?

What does this mean to you?

- He *"will convict the world concerning sin and righteousness and judgment; concerning sin, because they not believe in Me; and concerning righteousness, because I go to the Father and you no longer behold Me; and concerning judgment, because the ruler of this world has been judged"* (John 16:8-11).

Observation? What's the Spirit doing here?
What does this mean to you?

- *"These things I have spoken to you, while abiding with you. But the Helper, the Holy Spirit, whom the Father will send in My name, He will teach you all things, and bring to your remembrance all that I said to you"* (John 14:25-26, NASB).

  Observation? What's the Spirit doing here?
  What does this mean to you?

- *"I will ask the Father, and He will give you another Helper, that He may be with you forever"* (John 14:16, NASB). It's like spiritual adrenalin!

  Observation? What's the Spirit doing here?
  What does this mean to you?

- *"But I say walk by that which is spirit (reborn spirit), and you will not carry out the desire of that which is flesh. For the flesh sets its desire against that which is spirit, and that which is spirit sets its desire against the flesh"* (Galatians 5:16-17, authors' paraphrase).

  Observation? What's the Spirit doing here?
  What does this mean to you?

- The Spirit *"helps our weakness; for we do not know how to pray as we should, but the Spirit Himself intercedes for us with groanings too deep for words"* (Romans 8:26, NASB).

  Observation? What's the Spirit doing here?
  What does this mean to you?

- *"But if any of you lacks wisdom let him ask of God, who gives to all men generously and without criticism, and it will be given to him"* (James 1:5). Who gives the wisdom?

Observation? What's the Spirit doing here?
What does this mean to you?

- *"And we know that God causes all things to work together for good to those who love God, to those who are called according to His purpose"* (Romans 8:28, NASB). Who will work everything together with something else for good?

Observation? What's the Spirit doing here?
What does this mean to you?

- *"Now there are varieties of gifts, but the same Spirit. And there are varieties of ministries, and the same Lord. And there are varieties of effects, but the same God who works all things in all persons. But to each one is given the manifestation of the Spirit for the common good.... But one and the same Spirit works all these things, distributing to each one individually just as He wills"* (1 Corinthians 12:4-7,11, NASB).

Observation? What's the Spirit doing here?
What does this mean to you?

- *"He said to them, 'But who do you say that I am?' Simon Peter answered, 'You are the Christ, the Son of the living God.' And Jesus said to him, 'Blessed are you, Simon Barjona, because flesh and blood did not reveal this to you, but My Father who is in heaven' "* (Matthew 16:15-17, NASB). How will the Father reveal this answer about Jesus?

Observation? What's the Spirit doing here?
What does this mean to you?

- *"But if the Spirit of Him who raised Jesus from the dead dwells in you, He who raised Christ Jesus from the dead will also give life to your mortal bodies through His Spirit who dwells in you. So then, brethren, we are under obligation, not to the flesh, to live according to the flesh — for if you are living according to the flesh, you must die; but if by the Spirit you are putting to death the deeds of the body, you will live. <u>For all who are being led by the Spirit of God, these are sons of God</u>"* (Romans 8:11-14, NASB).

Observation? What's the Spirit doing here?
What does this mean to you?

FIVE STEPS TO EXPERIENCE THE PRESENCE OF JESUS

STEP #1: __Act as if__ Jesus is in you through the Holy Spirit.

STEP #2: __Believe__ that the power of the Holy Spirit permanently dwells in you to empower you.

STEP #3: __Count__ on the presence of Jesus through the Spirit to come through on your behalf. By the way, Jesus shows up when two or three gather in his name.

STEP #4: __Don't__ ask God to be with you; he already is! As long as you believe enough to follow Jesus, Jesus shows up and the Holy Spirit works for those and in those who believe in him. The presence of Jesus is with you and indwells inside you through the Holy Spirit. Instead of asking Jesus or the Spirit to come through on your behalf, thank them for being with you and in you forever!

STEP #5: __Expect__ Jesus to show up through his Spirit when two or three gather in the name of Jesus. ***"For where two or three have gathered together in My name, I am there in their midst"*** *(Matthew 18:20, NASB).*

Small groups provide the best opportunity for experiencing the presence of Jesus through the Spirit. This is precisely how Jesus unites, while everything else divides. We experience the presence of Jesus through the invisible power of the Spirit that dwells inside us.

 In what ways do you sense or experience the presence of Jesus?

Jesus is the physical presence of God, whom we follow. He is our Helper, our Comforter. Now that the physical presence of Jesus is no longer available to his followers, we have been given another Helper – another Comforter – who is the Spirit of God, the Holy Spirit.

"Now may the God of hope fill you with all joy and peace in believing, so that you will abound in hope by the power of the Holy Spirit." (Romans 15:13, NASB)

THE WAY

STUDY GUIDE 2: "FOLLOW!"

INTRODUCTION

STUDY GUIDE 2: "FOLLOW!" contains 6 Study Sessions:

Study Session #1 - The Revolutionary Call!

Study Session #2 - Three Requirements for Being a Disciple!

Study Session #3 - You Are the SALT of the Earth!

Study Session #4 - You Are the LIGHT of the World!

Study Session #5 - Three Habits of Following Jesus!

Study Session #6 - Five Ways to Show Jesus Off!

It's interesting to track the directions of Jesus to those who first came to him.

His first words can be summed up into two invitations from Jesus. The first is a simple invitation: **"Come and see!"** The interesting thing about getting to know Jesus is that you will find your experience with Jesus to be endless. His attractiveness and irresistibility are infinite.

We tend to want to prolong the "getting to know Jesus" process, organize our thoughts, systematize our beliefs, and require others who are curious to see Jesus through our eyes. This not only short-circuits the genuine process of seeing Jesus, it tends to move others to follow us and not Jesus.

Each person who is interested in seeing Jesus must see Jesus through his or her own eyes. After you have spent some initial time with Jesus, Jesus puts a second invitation right in front of you: "Follow me!" Once you get to know Jesus, he wants you to begin right away to follow in his steps.

Jesus repeatedly teaches how important it is to be a participant and not just another spectator. He urges anyone who hears his words to practice them — to act upon them. The beauty of doing your best to follow Jesus as soon as you get to know him is that you will find it natural to respond to him.

Once we've encountered Jesus, we have a strategic decision to make. Will we follow him or not? To choose to follow Jesus is the ultimate test of the genuineness of our relationship with Jesus.

A decision to follow Jesus begins with a single step forward, so let's get started together....

THE REVOLUTIONARY CALL!

From the beginning of his earthly ministry, Jesus expressed his most revolutionary call:

"Follow me" (Matthew 4:19; 8:22; 9:9; 10:38; 16:24; 19:21). Then, at the end of his time on earth, Jesus said, ***"Make disciples"** (Matthew 28:19).* A disciple is literally a learner – one who listens to and follows a teacher and his teachings. So, from beginning to end, it's really the same. Jesus invited people to follow him, and he wants his followers to invite others to follow him.

We see ourselves as simply followers of Jesus, not Christians or believers or Church members. We say it this way among our friends: "We're trying to do the most difficult thing we have ever done in our lives. We're doing our best to follow the teachings and principles of Jesus." This is discipleship or followership – to know Jesus and to make him known.

<u>Check out Jesus' first invitations to follow him.</u>

"Now as Jesus was walking by the Sea of Galilee, He saw two brothers, Simon who was called Peter, and Andrew his brother, casting a net into the sea; for they were fishermen. And He said to them, 'Follow Me, and I will make you fishers of men.' Immediately they left their nets and followed Him. Going on from there He saw two other brothers, James the son of Zebedee, and John his brother, in the boat with Zebedee their father, mending their nets; and He called them. Immediately they left the boat and their father, and followed Him." (Matthew 4:18-22, NASB)

 What kind of people are the first to be invited to follow Jesus?

What does Jesus mean by "fishers of men"? How would Jesus say it to you, if he were making a similar connection to your own work or role in life, asking you to follow him?

 Why do you think they made the decision to follow Jesus "immediately"?

A follower of Jesus must make it his or her single-minded focus to be like Jesus as best he can. Simply put, see and hear what Jesus does and do it!

THE PRIMARY MANDATE OF JESUS

The primary mandate of Jesus is for his followers to make followers (disciples) in all of the nations. *"All authority has been given to Me in heaven and on earth. Go therefore and <u>make disciples of all the nations</u>, baptizing them in the name of the Father and the Son and the Holy Spirit, teaching them to observe all that I commanded you; and lo, I am with you always, even to the end of the age"* (Matthew 28:18-20, NASB).

There is only one command from Jesus to his followers. It's not <u>to go</u> to the world, <u>to baptize</u> the world, or <u>to teach</u> the world. He doesn't command his followers to evangelize the world, proselytize, or convert the world. His command to his followers is simply and clearly to make disciples (followers) of him throughout the nations of the world. Once the command is stated, Jesus offers three participles (verbal descriptors) to carry out this command. The three participles are "<u>by going</u>," "<u>by baptizing</u>," and "<u>by teaching</u>."

Since we, most frequently, either miss or avoid the point that discipleship is making followers of Jesus in all of the nations (cultures) of the world, we tend to spend an excessive amount of time on the participles. Think of it! We focus so much on "going" as missionaries internationally, on short-term mission trips, and to a variety of outreach programs locally. But if you are going into the nations of the world without understanding it's all about Jesus, then you go and make it about all sorts of other things.

We tend to focus on "baptizing" everyone we can, without understanding that it is all about Jesus. We have baptized people into becoming Christians, Catholics, Baptists, Adventists, but this isn't the point of the baptizing Jesus is referring to here. Whatever else Jesus means by baptism, it isn't the process of identifying a person with any organization or religious affiliation; it's identifying a person as a follower of Jesus.

We focus on "teaching" people our particular doctrinal system that is not primarily about Jesus, but about ancillary thoughts and issues we deem important.

 Describe any of your experiences with going/baptizing/teaching. What impact did it have on you personally? Was there a secondary agenda or purpose involved, other than making disciples?

Jesus has a primary command: <u>make disciples</u>. Make disciples by going, baptizing, and teaching them to observe all I have taught you. Not only is there a tendency to skip over the command (make disciples) and to spend lots of energy in the participles (going, baptizing, and teaching), <u>there is also the tendency to reverse Jesus' approach</u>. We tend to reverse what Jesus is teaching. So, we <u>teach</u>, teach, teach, until a person is ready to be baptized, then we urge our well-taught, baptized believers <u>to go</u> out into the world.

Many times, the teaching, baptizing, and going is the end of the story, without ever getting to the original intent of Jesus – to make disciples of Jesus in all of the nations of the world.

Why do you think it is so easy to avoid the process of making disciples and to focus instead on more traditional programs and activities?

Here are six observations that outline the difficulties:

1. There is a need to be deprogrammed from what we've been taught. Most people who have grown up in a religious setting, have been programmed wrongly. Most believe the process of discipleship (making followers) is about passing on information. Therefore, the process of discipleship is always performed in the classroom — the better the information taught, the better the disciple. If we are going to make effective disciples, we must stop this kind of thinking. This approach tends to produce parrots, who can answer the questions and repeat the right words. However, personal transformation is lacking.

 Describe some of the more effective ways of learning that have worked for you in the past.

2. Discipleship is caught, not taught. Therefore, the process of discipleship takes lots of time. Jesus' process of discipleship was to take his disciples on a variety of field trips — outside the classroom. This allows a follower to observe, discuss, and ask questions along the way.

 If you went on an extended field trip with Jesus, what would you want to do, where would you want to go, and what would you want to talk about? How would you want to spend your time with him?

3. Discipleship is not one person teaching and a group listening. Discipleship requires participators, not spectators, for the process of discipleship to be effective. Jesus warned us not to call anyone "teacher" or "rabbi" or "father" or "leader" because of this misunderstanding. When followers come together, they gather to hear from one teacher – Jesus. Jesus is heard through the participants within the small group.

 How does participating in a small group help us teach one another?

4. Discipleship has only one object – one end game – Jesus. When Jesus commands his followers to make disciples of all nations, he is speaking of making followers of Jesus, himself. He is not saying to make all nations followers of Christianity or any other religious system. He is clearly saying to make all nations followers of Jesus.

These first four observations are difficult, but the next two may prove to be the most difficult of all.

5. Discipleship always takes more time than you think you have. This may discourage more people away from the process of discipleship than any other. It takes so much time! It's so much easier to teach a class, or to have a person read something, or to have people commit to memorize Bible verses or be able to articulate the major beliefs that your particular group has embraced. Discipleship is translating all you know and believe about Jesus into your lifestyle, day in and day out. Discipleship is embracing Jesus and his teachings in such a way that you are conversant about him.

For sure, the greatest difficulty to making disciples of all nations is this next one.

6. Discipleship must start with you. It starts with us. It starts with you! Unless you are a disciple, you have no way of entering into the process of discipleship with others. Are you a disciple – a follower of Jesus? You can be, if you want it.

 Which of these six difficulties is most true for you?

JESUS' CALL IS FOR SPIRITUAL TRANSFORMATION

Tamrat spent years of his life converting people to communism. Tim spent most of his life converting people to Christianity. Neither was able to generate spiritual transformation from the inside out, but only achieved an external degree of reformation. Communism or Christianity. That was our end game in life – to convert or change the world. We both came to the realization that we can't truly change a person, inside out. We have no power whatsoever to transform anyone!

If you think you must change the world, you will create an agenda for every person you approach. If a person is from a different religious or political persuasion, then your agenda is to talk them out of their religion or politics and into yours. If a person believes in evolution, then your agenda is to argue with him about creation. If a person is a socialist, then your agenda is to argue against capitalism. If a person is doing something you want him to change, then your agenda is to figure out a way to change that person. If you think you must change the world, you believe you are "right" and disrespect all others from different backgrounds. If you think you must change the world, then you may not include the only one who can change those in your world of influence – Jesus. If you think you must change the world, then you tend to think you are in charge of the results and actually making the changes happen! How silly and futile is that!

When we observe the life and teachings of Jesus, we see a very different approach. **Note** *this vital interaction between Jesus and his disciples:*

"When Jesus came to the region of Caesarea Philippi, he asked his disciples, 'Who do people say the Son of Man is?' They replied, 'Some say John the Baptist; others say Elijah; and still others, Jeremiah or one of the prophets.' 'But what about you?' he asked. 'Who do you say I am?' Simon Peter answered, 'You are the Messiah, the Son of the living God.' Jesus replied, <u>'Blessed are you, Simon son of Jonah, for this was not revealed to you by flesh and blood, but by my Father in heaven.</u> And I tell you that you are Peter, and on this rock I will build my church, and the gates of death will not overcome it.' " (Matthew 16:13-18, NIV)

NOTE no one taught Peter that Jesus was the Messiah, the Son of the living God, but the Father revealed this to him. Only God can do this. This is genuine spiritual transformation. You can't do it; only God can!

NOTE who it is who supernaturally draws people to Jesus: *" 'Stop grumbling among yourselves,' Jesus answered. 'No one can come to me unless the Father who sent me draws them, and I will raise them up at the last day. It is written in the Prophets: "They will all be taught by God." Everyone who has heard the Father and learned from him comes to me' "* (John 6:43-45).

If God is the one who reveals to people who Jesus is and actually draws them to Jesus, then it is God who is doing any converting work. And, if God is the only one who can do the converting of a person's life, then what role do we play in the process? It seems the end game of the Father is to draw to Jesus and reveal Jesus to those who have ears to hear and eyes to see.

 How might this understanding change your role in the process of converting others? What is your role and what do you think is God's role in this process?

As followers of Jesus, what ought our end game be? Two observations come to mind.

FIRST: <u>The Father has already taken the role of converting people, therefore we are not to be into the conversion business.</u> **NOTE** the Father has no interest in converting anyone to become a part of any religious system or theological set of beliefs. His end game is converting — transforming their lives to be related to Jesus. The Father's end game is all about Jesus.

SECOND: <u>Since we are not responsible for the other person's conversion, our job is to introduce Jesus to all who are interested in him.</u> Followers of Jesus need to focus on advancing the conversation of Jesus in every way we can. We are not to concern ourselves whether someone is a Baptist, Buddhist, Christian, Catholic, or Muslim; the end game for all followers of Jesus is to introduce people to Jesus. We are to make this our total and only agenda.

At the end of the gospel of John Jesus has an intriguing encounter with Peter.

" 'Truly, truly, I say to you, when you were younger, you used to gird yourself and walk wherever you wished; but when you grow old, you will stretch out your hands and someone else will gird you, and bring you where you do not wish to go.' Now this He said, signifying by what kind of death he would glorify God. And when He had spoken this, He said to him, 'Follow Me!' " (John 21:18-19, NASB)

Jesus shares with Peter how his life is going to change as he ages. Peter is going to grow old, will have to be dressed, and will be led around by others, rather than being able to go and do the things he wants to do. After he shared this end of life scenario for Peter, Jesus gave him the best advice: ***"Follow me!"*** Then Peter looked up and saw John nearby and became concerned about John's end of life story.

"Peter, turning around, saw the disciple whom Jesus loved following them. . . . So Peter seeing him said to Jesus, 'Lord, and what about this man?' Jesus said to him, 'If I want him to remain until I come, what is that to you? You follow Me!' " (John 21:20-22, NASB)

At the beginning of the encounter with Peter, Jesus simply commanded Peter to follow him. Now, after Peter pointed out John, Jesus basically says to Peter, **"What's going to happen to John is none of your business."** Then, Jesus emphatically says to Peter, not just "follow me," but, **"<u>You, on your part, follow me!</u>"**

 Do you believe that God's plan for other people is truly none of your business?

Jesus emphasizes twice what he wants from Peter and from you and me: <u>FOLLOW ME</u>! These are the two words that have become the most powerful words in all of recorded history. There are three descriptions that come up for me here.

<u>Transformational:</u> FOLLOW ME and you will be changed from the inside out!

<u>Revolutionary:</u> FOLLOW ME and I will turn the world upside down as I turn you right side up!

<u>Single-minded:</u> FOLLOW ME and everything else will be taken care of.
This is truly Jesus plus nothing!

Don't get caught up in anyone else's walk with Jesus. Pay special attention to your relationship with Jesus. Nothing else nor anyone else is your business, until you are focused on your business with your best friend, Jesus.

 What did the disciples do during their time with Jesus that allowed God to work out his conversion process of revealing Jesus to them?

In order for God to do his work in your life, what must you do?

IF YOU CHOOSE TO FOLLOW, BEWARE OF THE BATTLE

If you respond to Jesus' revolutionary call to follow him, you must realize you are enlisting in the principal revolutionary war of the ages. This is <u>a reality</u>!

The Reality and Requirement of the Battle

The battle motif is not only a reality; it's a requirement for learning to follow Jesus. As you follow in the steps of Jesus, you will notice what the Spirit actually led him to do. Immediately after John baptized Jesus, the Spirit led him into the wilderness to be tempted. This temptation was a testing to prove his genuineness. Check it out:

"<u>Jesus, full of the Holy Spirit, returned from the Jordan and was led around by the Spirit in the wilderness for forty days, being tempted by the devil</u>. And He ate nothing during those days, and when they had ended, He became hungry. And the devil said to Him, 'If You are the Son of God, tell this stone to become bread.' And Jesus answered him, 'It is written, "Man shall not live on bread alone." '

"And he led Him up and showed Him all the kingdoms of the world in a moment of time. And the devil said to Him, 'I will give You all this domain and its glory; for it has been handed over to me, and I give it to whomever I wish. Therefore <u>if You worship before me, it shall all be Yours</u>.' Jesus answered him, 'It is written, "You shall worship the Lord your God and serve Him only." '

"And he led Him to Jerusalem and had Him stand on the pinnacle of the temple, and said to Him, '<u>If You are the Son of God, throw Yourself down from here</u>; for it is written, "He will command His angels concerning You to guard You," and, "On their hands they will bear You up, So that You will not strike Your foot against a stone." ' And Jesus answered and said to him, 'It is said, "You shall not put the Lord your God to the test." ' " (Luke 4:1-12, NASB)

To confirm your character and the genuineness of who you are, you will discover several tests. This has the effect of a crucible to prove out your new relationship with Jesus. It's within this crucible effect that you must learn to follow Jesus with your whole heart. This is not the time to learn more; it's the time to put into action the little that you know. This crucible effect has become a psychological and spiritual "right of passage" in order to prepare a person for living life on purpose.

The three temptations thrown at Jesus by the devil are universal to all who wish to follow in the footsteps of Jesus. **(1)** "Tell this stone to become bread." **(2)** "If you bow down and worship me, you can have power over the kingdoms of the world." **(3)** "Jump off this high pinnacle, for God will save you."

✎ **How do you identify with each temptation? What does each mean to you?**

(1) **"Tell this stone to become bread."**

(2) **"If you bow down and worship me, you can have power over the kingdoms of the world."**

(3) **"Jump off this high pinnacle, for God will save you."**

And, what was common about each of Jesus' responses?

Do you ever feel as if you are engaged in spiritual battle with evil?

 What can you take away from Jesus' encounter that you can personally apply in your own spiritual battles? (What to do and not to do.)

NOTE how Luke ends this section regarding the battle with the devil:

"When the devil had finished every temptation, he left Him until an opportune time." (Luke 4:13, NASB)

 What does this comment from Luke mean to you about your own battle?

HOW FOLLOWING JESUS CHANGES THE WORLD

The Kingdom of God and the Kingdom of heaven are used interchangeably. Even though Jesus teaches so little on the church (mentions it twice), he spends lots of time teaching about the Kingdom. Today the Kingdom concept has escaped our notice, even though Jesus places so much emphasis on it. It's not that the Kingdom has been rejected, but reduced. In general we reduce the Kingdom of God to our particular flavor of the faith we have embraced. There's a belief that what we have embraced is the right way and therefore we must carry our particular form of faith and system of beliefs to the rest of the world. The Kingdom is so much greater than the particular faith or system you have embraced. Jesus is referring to the Kingdom of God, not the kingdom of the Catholics or the Protestants or the Muslims or the Buddhists.

The way Jesus teaches it, <u>the Kingdom is greater than anything that has ever existed on earth</u>. Jesus makes it clear that the Kingdom is near, here and among us right now, yet there also seems to be a time in the future, when the Kingdom will be fully experienced on earth.

<u>Jesus and the Kingdom offer the only possible solution to transforming the culture.</u> There are three things about Jesus and the Kingdom that are most attractive and most effective in changing any society:

FIRST: <u>Character.</u> <u>There is no one who ever lived who has ever surpassed the character standard that Jesus set</u>. He set the bar so high that he is revered in every culture of the world. Jesus, the King of his Kingdom, is the only moral authority with any kind of power to change society. Although many Christian leaders today at the highest levels present the Church as God's plan – God's solution – to change the world, this thinking is way too narrow and is the opposite to what Jesus taught.

Sometimes the Church is effective and sometimes it's not. Leaders are often morally good and leaders are sometimes morally flawed. So, at any given time, the Church will not be able to deliver a moral authority to the community. But the Kingdom is constant. Its power and effectiveness depend upon its leader – Jesus. Therefore living in the Kingdom and inviting others to share in it is the only solution to transforming a broken culture. This isn't criticizing the organized Church, but only recognizing Jesus had a bigger and better idea in the Kingdom.

 What is the difference to you between representing the Church and representing the Kingdom?

How would this difference impact your relationships with the people you share Jesus with?

SECOND: Fulfillment and meaning. Jesus is the ultimate standard and the Kingdom is the lifestyle of living out his standard in society. <u>The lifestyle of Kingdom living is where ultimate fulfillment and meaning reside</u>. They are the laws of the universe. You cannot break the laws of the Kingdom, but they can break you. For instance, one of the laws of the Kingdom is to forgive those who have hurt you. If you refuse to live out this Kingdom principle, you will pay dearly for it. You will be bound by your lack of forgiveness. You will be eaten up with this unforgiving heart. By breaking the principle, you are broken. <u>When living within the Kingdom, you are safe and free and most fulfilled</u>.

 What assurance does this give you concerning the unbreakable nature of the Kingdom principles?

THIRD: God. <u>Where better to discover a personal relationship with the God of gods than where Jesus lives in his Kingdom</u>. If God were to take on human flesh and live among us on this earth, he would most certainly say the things that Jesus said and do the things that Jesus did. **If you follow the teachings and principles of Jesus, along the way you will find the God of the universe**.

<u>Follow the King and you'll discover the Kingdom; embrace the Kingdom lifestyle and you'll discover the King</u>. The Kingdom is the only thing Jesus calls the Gospel – the Gospel (Good News) of the Kingdom. When you become more conversant with the Kingdom, you will come to know that this is not only the Good News; it is the BEST NEWS ever – all in Jesus.

This is why we affirmatively answer Jesus' call: "FOLLOW ME!"

THREE REQUIREMENTS FOR BEING A DISCIPLE!

TO BE LIKE JESUS

A disciple – a learner and follower of Jesus – must make it his or her single-minded focus to be like Jesus as best he can. Simply put, see and hear what Jesus does and do it! In order to be a true follower or disciple of Jesus – to be like Jesus – it's important to understand the leadership style of Jesus. Once you understand this, you can follow him more effectively.

There are three basic dimensions to the leadership style of Jesus that are vital to embrace.

FIRST: It's personal and powerful! Jesus was God in the flesh – the *incarnational dimension* of his leadership style. In the same way Jesus fleshed out the invisible God we are to flesh out or incarnate – to make alive – Jesus. We are essentially to be Jesus in all that we do. We do this by seeking to know him better in all we do – to include Jesus in every decision, every meeting, and every relationship. We do this by practicing the presence of Jesus every day – walking, talking, thinking, and loving like Jesus. We miss the power in knowing Jesus when we ignore his presence and avoid his pain. Remember Paul's words: ***"That I may know Him and the power of His resurrection and the fellowship of His sufferings"*** (Philippians 3:10 , NASB).

SECOND: The leadership style of Jesus is relational and relevant! Jesus made it clear that there is no genuine relationship with him without being in relationship with others. This is the leadership dimension of interdependence, connection, and compassion. He demonstrated this relational dimension when he chose the first three disciples to be with him – just to be with him in relationship, in community. When you isolate yourself, you short-change yourself and others in the family of Jesus. When you embrace interdependence with Jesus and others, you exchange your life to know the power of God. You can actually experience his power in this community.

THIRD: The leadership style of Jesus is also underground and invisible! This is the s*ecret dimension* of Jesus' leadership style you are to follow that will generate real impact, accomplishment, and creativity in the world around you. His ways are just not the normal ways of man. His own disciples, in much of what he tried to do, opposed him. They tried to push aside the woman who had a bleeding problem. They wanted to send the 5,000 away for them to fend for themselves rather than feed them. They viewed the man born blind with a certain disregard. They had given up on any possibility of Jesus doing anything helpful for his friend Lazarus.

The leadership style of Jesus is personal and relational, but it's also invisible. How do you think you might be able to personally relate to Jesus and to others, yet remain "invisible" while you do so?

We resist Jesus as well, mostly by ignoring him. We tend toward creating and producing the visible things; Jesus was and is totally into the invisible, under the radar, approach to serving others. This is real impact — really making a difference in the world around you.

> *To walk, talk, think, love, and bleed like Jesus is the focus and goal of the disciple. Living your life in this way means that you will be a radical. "Radical" means getting to the root or operating from the basic fundamentals of life; it's following the principles that make life work best.*

The key to being a disciple is learning and practicing how to be Jesus in everything you do and wherever you are. You see, Jesus doesn't want you to **demonstrate for him** (that's the easy thing to do); he wants you to **demonstrate him** as you walk like he walked, talk like he talked, think as he thought, love as he loved, and even give yourself to sacrificially bleed as Jesus bled for the world. That is being a disciple of Jesus — doing the toughest thing you'll ever do in your life, to follow the teachings and principles of the irresistible and attractive Jesus.

THE MASTER PLAN OF DISCIPLESHIP

Jesus made it clear what he expected his early followers to do. At the very end of Matthew's gospel Jesus says, *"All authority in heaven and on earth has been given to me. Therefore go and make disciples of all nations, baptizing them in the name of the Father and of the Son and of the Holy Spirit, and teaching them to obey everything I have commanded you. And surely I am with you always, to the very end of the age"* (Matthew 28:18-20, NIV).

Whatever else can be taught from this passage, it's important that you see what was on Jesus' heart in these last words for his followers. Jesus presents one command here; it's not an option. Jesus is making it clear that he wants his followers to make disciples of all nations. Make disciples of <u>all</u> nations!

A disciple is literally a learner — one who listens and follows a teacher and his teachings. Jesus commands his disciples to go make disciples of all nations. "Nations" is best understood as cultures. We're realizing that no matter what culture is introduced to Jesus, the response is amazingly positive and transformational. And just as Jesus gave this command to his first disciples, it's clear that Jesus wants all of his disciples everywhere to continue to multiply more disciples.

Now, the term "disciple" is only used in the Gospels; it cannot be found in the rest of the New Testament. It's like the Gospels are filled with urging all to become disciples and the letters to the many fellowships of Jesus in the New Testament are filled with practicing what it means to be a disciple.

A disciple is simply a follower of Jesus — one who hears his teachings and seeks to practice them. We are doing our best to be faithful disciples of Jesus and to obey Jesus by making disciples of Jesus everywhere we go. We see ourselves as followers of Jesus, not Christians or believers or Church members. We say it this way among our friends: "We're doing the most difficult thing we have ever done in our lives. We're doing our best to follow the teachings and principles of Jesus." This is discipleship — to know Jesus and to make him known.

We've come to realize that the master plan of discipleship is a two-way street and there is an order to it. Jesus first initiates the master plan, himself. Jesus is the one who initiates the discipleship relationship by calling people to himself. He invites all who are interested to follow him. In a very real sense, disciples aren't made; they are called.

Not only does Jesus initiate the discipleship relationship, Jesus is a major believer in the disciples he is calling. Check this out: **Jesus sent his disciples across the Sea of Galilee, directly into a storm**. Then Jesus shows up in the midst of the storm, walking on water, ready to calm the storm and save the disciples. *They feared he was a ghost and Jesus said, " 'Take courage, it is I; do not be afraid.' Peter said to Him, 'Lord, if it is You, command me to come to You on the water.' And He said, 'Come!' And Peter got out of the boat, and walked on the water and came toward Jesus"* (Matthew 14:27-29, NASB).

NOTE what happens here. Jesus is not the only one who ever walked on water. Peter also actually walked on water, too. Jesus invited Peter to step out of the boat and walk on water to him. Peter did it! It was amazing, until Peter took his eyes off of Jesus and became distracted by his circumstances.

"But seeing the wind, he became frightened, and beginning to sink, he cried out, 'Lord, save me!' Immediately Jesus stretched out His hand and took hold of him, and said to him, 'You of little faith, why did you doubt?' When they got into the boat, the wind stopped."
(Matthew 14:30-32, NASB)

Did you get that?

He scolds Peter for doubting his ability to continue to walk on the water to Jesus. Here's what seems to be happening. When Jesus calls you to himself, he is a believer in you. Jesus believes you can do it, as you keep your focus on him. Jesus calls you to follow him and believes you are able to do great things in this new partnership with him. He doesn't call you to watch him, but to follow in his steps!

 Would it change your trust of Jesus' leadership in your life to know that he believes in you and believes you can do what he asks as long as you focus on him?

THE DISCIPLE'S SIDE OF THE STREET

The master plan of discipleship is a two-way street – Jesus' side of the street and the disciple's side. Jesus initiates an invitation to all who are interested to follow him and believes each one can do it. The disciple's side of the street is found in his or her response to Jesus. The disciple must respond to the invitation extended by Jesus. Here's what the disciple's side of the street might look like.

FIRST: <u>Being a disciple is to have a teachable spirit and a heart for God</u>. If you are a disciple, you will work on being a learner. You don't already have it all figured out. You are coming to Jesus as a little child.

SECOND: <u>Being a disciple is to be holy – set apart unto God for his mission</u>. When you are set apart in this way, you will be going against the grain – a contrarian, but you will be walking hand in hand with Jesus and that's the only way to get through the piles of life anyway.

THIRD: <u>Being a disciple means to enhance your self-esteem</u>. Knowing whose you are, will determine who you are. When you understand clearly how centering and empowering it is to follow Jesus, he becomes the key to your self-esteem.

FOURTH: <u>Being a disciple means to confirm your calling – your purpose in life</u>. When you follow Jesus, you will know the reason why you are here on planet earth and you will have a great opportunity to act it out.

FIFTH: <u>Being a disciple means to manage your conflicts</u>. When following Jesus, your conflicts become opportunities for making a difference and learning more about yourself.

SIXTH: <u>Being a disciple means to be able to express your personal faith</u>. One of the common problems believers have is to be able to share their faith. All kinds of training materials and methodologies have been produced over the years, but there is nothing more effective in communicating your faith than being a follower of Jesus plus nothing. It's contagious! The only message you can share with credibility is your own personal experience, strength, and hope you are finding in Jesus.

SEVENTH: <u>Being a disciple means to make disciples</u>. If you are a disciple, then you will multiply yourself. You will make other disciples of Jesus as you live your life. You won't be able to stop it! Jesus will shine through!

EIGHTH: <u>Being a disciple means to know Jesus better</u>. Being a disciple is all about knowing Jesus. In fact, I'm convinced that this may be the only real goal for anything we ever do – in your home, in your vocation, on your vacation, as you parent your children, and when you come together as a group of people in the name of Jesus.

Paul, who was apprehended by Jesus on the road to Damascus, expressed how important knowing Jesus better really is: *"I consider everything a loss because of the surpassing worth of knowing Christ Jesus my Lord, for whose sake I have lost all things. I consider them garbage that I may gain Christ and be found in him, not having a righteousness of my own that comes from the law, but that which is through faith in Christ – the righteousness that comes from God on the basis of faith"* (Philippians 3:8-9, NIV).

 What comes up for you as you think of how you might learn to know Jesus better?

DISCIPLESHIP IS A SINGLE-MINDED FOCUS

Most of the time we have in our minds that the disciples of Jesus were only the Twelve he chose. But as you examine the life and teachings of Jesus, you will come across several references to a much larger group of disciples or followers of Jesus.

Crowds of people followed Jesus as he moved from village to village. Naturally, many of these were just curious, but there were also quite a few who were taking Jesus seriously and desiring to get in line and follow him. I'm sure there were a variety of definitions in Jesus' time as to what it meant to be a disciple. It's still a very relevant question requiring repeated and fresh examination today.

As we make our way through some thoughts on what it means to be a disciple of Jesus, it's important to take him at his word on the subject before making things up on our own. At one point in his ministry, Jesus turned to the many who were following him and challenged them to be his true disciples. He presented three very tough requirements in order to be a disciple who claims to be a follower of him.

In the 14th chapter of Luke's gospel, he records all three of these requirements during one dramatic scene where crowds were following Jesus everywhere he went.

REQUIREMENT #1 – PRIORITY

"Now as Jesus proceeded on his journey, great crowds accompanied him and he turned and spoke to them, 'If anyone comes to me without setting aside his relationship with his father and mother and wife and children and brothers and sisters, and even his own life, he cannot be a disciple of mine.' " (Luke 14:25-26, authors' paraphrase)

Jesus declares the first prerequisite to be one of his disciples – the requirement of priority. There are many reasons people might follow Jesus, but if you want to be a disciple of Jesus, it is necessary to make Jesus your number one, above-all-others, priority. He makes it tougher than just saying that he wants to be your best friend after your family members. He requires that you set aside your family members – father, mother, wife, children, brothers and sisters – to amplify his importance over all natural relationships. By comparison, Jesus is above all relationships in priority. You go to him first!

He makes it even more personal when he says to set aside *"even* [your] *own life."* Jesus wants you to place him above all of your own self-interests. This is the area where we create many of our own little gods that we come to worship and put ahead of or equal to Jesus. You cannot be full of yourself and at the same time be acting as a disciple – a follower of Jesus. There is not enough room in your heart for that type of balancing act.

In most translations, Jesus is quoted as saying that he is requiring you to hate your family and to hate yourself. Jesus spoke in Aramaic and in that language the wording is clearly not "hate," but to "set aside" all others to put Jesus in first place or in the very center of your life.

Then, note that Jesus doesn't equivocate at all here. He says unless you put him up as the highest priority in your life — the highest position of authority — you cannot be his disciple. It's not that you cannot be a good disciple or one of the better disciples or a better than average disciple; it's that you cannot be a disciple of Jesus at all. There is very little wiggle room here.

So, do you want to be a disciple of Jesus? Then, you must make Jesus your number one, above-all-others person you go to — the one you consult first and the one you imitate most. Jesus wants you to walk with him so closely that you don't start your day, enter into a meeting, begin a conversation, respond to a crisis, react to an enemy, or end your day without talking with him first. This is the requirement of priority!

 Will you take this challenge from Jesus and make him your priority, starting today? What does that mean for you?

REQUIREMENT #2 – PERSEVERANCE

The first requirement to be a disciple or follower of Jesus is to make him your highest priority of life. Jesus now declares the second prerequisite to be one of his disciples – <u>the requirement of perseverance. The requirement of perseverance is to continue to follow Jesus no matter what happens to you</u>. Your relationship with Jesus is your highest priority and you will not be deterred in following him and shaping your life after him by anything. You will hang in there no matter what!

Here's how Jesus states this requirement:

"The man who will not carry his cross and follow in my footsteps cannot be my disciple."
(Luke 14:27, authors' paraphrase)

Jesus' disciple must carry the cross just as Jesus did – following in the footsteps of Jesus. If you are unwilling to do this, then you cannot be his disciple.

So, what does it mean to carry the cross? The cross of Jesus is the greatest expression of sacrificial love ever. Here is God's Messiah – the Son of the living God and the most powerful person ever born – and his ultimate act was a demonstration of love, not power. The Roman Empire's symbol was the cross – an emblem of domination and power, because of their method of discipline – crucifixion. Jesus literally turned the cross upside down and inside out to turn this scary symbol of domination and power into the ultimate symbol of sacrificial love.

The disciples were looking for God's Messiah to overthrow Roman domination and power. They believed that would be the appropriate game plan for the Messiah, so they were expecting some powerful moves by Jesus on their behalf against the Romans. This is why they just didn't hear it or didn't want to believe it when Jesus announced his Messianic plan. His plan was to demonstrate the love of God to the world by allowing himself to die on that Roman cross – transforming the terrifying symbol of the cross into a symbol of hope, peace, and grace. Now that's the greatest example of sacrificial love ever, and it triggered the Jesus movement that has transformed more lives and cultures than any other movement in all of history.

 So, what does it mean FOR YOU to carry the cross?

I think it has to do with identifying your mission in life so much with Jesus that you actually incarnate him – or flesh him out. Carrying the cross is to be a sacrificial lover – to be Jesus in all you say and do.

Normally, when Jesus talks about the cross and discipleship, he uses the word to "take up" the cross. Luke uses a different word here. He uses the word that means to carry or bear the cross as opposed to take up or pick up your cross. The term Luke uses is not something you carry, but something that is attached to you. It's the same term Luke uses when he talks about Paul's mission to bear the name of Jesus to the Gentiles, their kings, and to the house of Israel. Note what Jesus says here: ***"I will show him how much he must suffer for my name"*** (Acts 9:16, NIV). When you bear the name of Jesus, you will also suffer the shame of the cross.

Paul also used this term when he wrote to the followers of Jesus in Galatia, when he says, ***"From now on, let no one make trouble for me; for I carry the marks of Jesus branded on my body"*** *(Galatians 6:17, authors' paraphrase).* Paul was so identified with Jesus by the scars and marks he had received while following him. He carried this identification with him wherever he went. He didn't have to pick it up; it was already attached to him.

When you carry the cross, you are actually so identified with Jesus that you are to be Jesus to the world around you. It's to be proactive with the love of Jesus rather than reactive against whatever or whoever assaults you.

So, are you willing to identify with Jesus by carrying his cross and the embarrassment of it?

There is a cost factor in carrying your cross. Following Jesus as your highest priority and fleshing him out in your life will stir up lots of controversy for you. When you take the path of Jesus versus the normal ways of religious living, you will suffer the consequences. One of these consequences is that you will be excommunicated from your religious society and community. Being like Jesus, choosing the sacrificial love approach, will most certainly separate you from most religious people, because you are like Jesus, a contrarian – going against the grain.

Another consequence of carrying your cross is that you must endure everything that is thrown at you – trials, troubles, stresses, injustices, and all kinds of things that will require you to give of yourself in a sacrificial way. When you think you can't take it any longer, you still hang on. It's the requirement of perseverance – hanging in there with Jesus no matter what!

REQUIREMENT #3 – POSSESSIONS

This final requirement Jesus presents to the crowd may be the toughest of all. Before he actually presents it, Jesus offers two illustrations that strongly urge you to count the cost of what it means to follow Jesus. The first has to do with the building of a tower: *"If any of you wanted to build a tower, wouldn't he first sit down and work out the cost of it to see if he can afford to finish it? Otherwise, when he has laid the foundation and found himself unable to complete the building, everyone who sees it will begin to jeer at him, saying, 'This is the man who started to build a tower but couldn't finish it!' "* (Luke 14:28-30).

Then, Jesus illustrates counting the cost with a king going off to war against another king: *"Or, suppose there is a king who is going to war with another king, doesn't he sit down first and consider whether he can engage the twenty thousand of the other king with his own ten thousand? And if he decides he can't, then while the other king is still a long way off, he sends messengers to him to ask for conditions of peace"* (Luke 14:31-32).

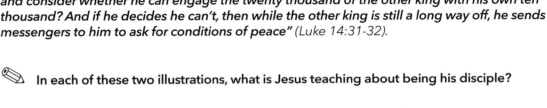 In each of these two illustrations, what is Jesus teaching about being his disciple?

 What examples from your own life do you have in which you "counted the cost" before making your decision? Did it help?

Then Jesus reveals his third requirement:

"So it is with you; only the man who says goodbye to all his possessions can be my disciple." (Luke 14:33, authors' paraphrase)

Many of your translations say something like this: **"In the same way, those of you who do not give up everything you have cannot be my disciples."** Naturally, the wording "give up everything" is the operative phrase here. What does it mean to give up everything? The first translation seems to read best: **"Say goodbye to all of your possessions."** That says it well! The Greek word here means to "take leave" or "renounce" your possessions.

Jesus is not saying that you are <u>to give over</u> all your possessions, but <u>to give them up</u>. This is renouncing the ownership of all you have. You really don't own what you have. You are a manager or steward of what God has allowed you to collect. Jesus wants you to realize this and be willing to give up your personal ownership of all you have for Jesus and the Kingdom. Jesus wants you to hold on to your stuff, but hold it loosely and be ready to share generously as it is needed.

It's even more than this. <u>You are not just to give up everything you have, but all you are as well – your very existence</u>. This is built into the word used for possessions. He owns it all – you and all of your stuff! It's learning to wear the cloak of materialism loosely and to live your life as one who is owned and directed by Jesus. So, make Jesus your highest priority over all relationships, make him your priority no matter what, and renounce the ownership of all you are and have. These are the requirements of being a disciple of Jesus.

Note the progression of the three requirements Jesus is looking for. You must make Jesus your highest priority, then you must continue to make him your priority no matter what – perseverance – and then all you have must be given up to Jesus for his use. With these three requirements in place, Jesus says you are now eligible to be his disciple.

<u>The spirit of these discipleship requirements is all about surrender – abandoning all competing relationships and securities for Jesus and the Kingdom</u>. There are many examples of surrender with both good and bad results. Peter, James, and John left their fishing business to follow Jesus full-time. Levi left his position at the local tax collections office. Then there is the rich young ruler who was unwilling to renounce his wealth and follow Jesus. He walked away with great sadness. Paul didn't leave his profession of making tents, but was able to take it with him wherever he went. Being a disciple of Jesus is one of the most amazing adventures ever.

 Do you want to be a disciple of Jesus? To make him your priority, to follow him no matter what, and to renounce ownership of your life? What's holding you back from this kind of surrender?

What's interesting is that the more closely you follow alongside Jesus the easier it is to live as a disciple. He gets you and you get him. What a deal!

YOU ARE THE **SALT** OF THE EARTH!

In the early public teaching of Jesus, he set the record straight about what his radical message was all about.

In a very real sense, Jesus was answering the obvious question his audience was asking of him: ***"Jesus, how does your teaching differ from what we've been taught?"***

- His message was revolutionary and not the same old thing.
- His message was transformational – life changing.
- His message was counter-intuitive and unexpected.
- His message was spoken with authority. He didn't quote other rabbis or authorities. He presented himself as the authority.

Within this message of Jesus we will find the most foundational seeds for living our lives most effectively! This kind of message takes time to absorb, so take the time for yourself. Ask, "How does Jesus' teaching differ from what we've been taught?"

Jesus unites people from all cultural, religious, and social backgrounds. Jesus unites people from different nations, people from various parent-child relationships, Moslems, Christians, and Jews. We invite you to see Jesus without layers of man-made traditions, rules, and expectations, making him approachable to everyone.

Jesus described what it means to be a happy, blessed, and fulfilled follower and he uses two dynamic roles to position his followers in this world – salt and light. The first is, ***"You are the salt of the earth. But if the salt loses its saltiness, how can it be made salty again? It is no longer good for anything, except to be thrown out and trampled underfoot"*** (Matthew 5:13, NIV).

 What comes to mind when you think of yourself as being salt?

Jesus says, **"You are the salt of the earth!"** It's not that you might be or you could be, but you are. Salt was used as a preservative to counteract the decay in meat. In order for salt to be effective it must be out of the saltshaker and applied to the meat.

<u>Salt is like the invisible presence of God</u>. <u>It must be sensed</u>. You're the salt in the world around you – the invisible presence of God among those you touch. Just by your presence there is to be a preserving of purity, honesty, and fairness.

A saltless disciple is good for nothing except to be thrown out and trampled underfoot. Jesus uses the term tasteless. The original Greek word is moraino, which means to be foolish – to play the fool, insipid, dull, flat, or deficient.

In rabbinic literature, salt is associated with wisdom – a foolish disciple has no impact on his world. Also, salt adds flavor to things. Jesus is to life what salt is to food. Jesus and the Kingdom lend flavor to life to be a difference-maker. Flavoring it with your salt-like presence changes the world.

It was Saint Francis of Assisi who said, "Preach the gospel at all times, and when necessary use words." This is precisely what it means to be salt – invisibly effective.

The first four beatitudes describe what it means to be **SALT – your heart relationship before God**.

The second four beatitudes describe what it means to be **LIGHT – your heart relationship before God as felt and seen by others**.

Let's check out all eight beatitudes as snapshots of what Jesus views as a blessed and happy Kingdom lifestyle.

We come now to the most amazing seminar/workshop Jesus ever taught. Jesus has already begun to do wonderful things in healing and touching the lives of so many in his new ministry among them as the new Rabbi in town. He has already chosen a few men to follow him – to be taught in his way. So here is where the question automatically arises: "Jesus, how does your teaching differ from all of the other Rabbis' teaching that we have grown up with? How does your teaching compare with what we've been taught?"

This is the question for every one of us, no matter from which culture or religious background we were brought up. HOW DO THE TEACHINGS OF JESUS DIFFER FROM WHAT I'VE BEEN TAUGHT SO FAR? Jesus sets out to answer this underlying question among the people and it is recorded in Matthew 5-7. These are the most dynamic chapters in the New Testament and possibly the most revolutionary!

POOR IN SPIRIT

It all begins right here: ***"Blessed are the poor in spirit , for theirs is the kingdom of heaven"*** *(Matthew 5:3, NIV)*. You are blessed if you have this quality of being poor in spirit. The term "poor in spirit" is a word that means that you must beg in order to live. You are that desperate! It's having a right evaluation of yourself before God. He's God and self-sufficient and I am not! In order to embrace each of these beatitudes it seems best to me to re-articulate each into a discipline or an action step.

With "poor in spirit," you as the discipline are to REAFFIRM YOUR POVERTY. Jesus is speaking to a massive group of people who have been taught by some of the most haughty men who have spent their lives outlining what it means to be right or righteous before God, and that system is really a performance system of attempting some level of perfection. Jesus begins at the very opposite end of the spectrum. Righteousness begins when you understand your total need for God – your spiritual poverty!

 What meaning does "spiritual poverty" have for you?

To reaffirm your spiritual poverty means to have a right evaluation of yourself before self, God, and others. All of life begins right at this point. Possessing a right evaluation of yourself before self, God, and others is true humility – the exact opposite of the blindness of pride. Pride is one of the seven deadly sins; it's universal among humans and it's devastating! Pride always seeks to be exalted, to be first, and to be praised. (Don't misunderstand! There is a good sense that some people identify as pride, such as self-confidence or self-satisfaction. But it does seem helpful to call it just that – self-confidence or self-satisfaction.) Pride blinds you so that you don't see yourself for who you are becoming, pride causes you to position others in a crippled, weakened condition, and pride causes you to begin to think that you may be God – the center of the universe.

Pride is not always obvious. It's an insidious cancer that skews your thinking, distances you from enjoying your relationships, and sets you up for a fall in whatever you do. Reaffirming your spiritual poverty is the recognition of your spiritual bankruptcy. It's coming to grips with your humanity! Pride can show itself with the simple thought that you handled your life today without God. It's an optical problem – the big "I."

 What are some of the less obvious ways that you struggle with pride in your life?

NOTE ONE MORE THING: Those who are poor in spirit are the ones who will receive the Kingdom of heaven. Only two of the eight snapshots reference the Kingdom – the first and the last. The Kingdom belongs to those who know and admit their need for God. It all starts here. You see, it's only when you come to the end of yourself (poor in spirit) that you finally realize that God is enough. So, reaffirm your spiritual poverty without God and you will become richer than you ever imagined.

 So, how would you define "poor in spirit"?

 What does this have to do with being blessed or happy?

MOURNING

We started with **"Blessed are the poor in spirit, for theirs is the kingdom of heaven."** The discipline for this Kingdom snapshot is to <u>REAFFIRM YOUR POVERTY</u> — to have a right evaluation of yourself before God — your wickedness (making it possible to do almost anything, any time), and your wonder (you are not as bad as you could be, since you are created in the image of the God of gods).

Now, we come to the second beatitude: **"Blessed are those who mourn, for they will be comforted"** (Matthew 5:4, NIV). Now wait a minute! Blessed are those who mourn? Are you kidding? How can mourning be a blessed experience or one that makes you happy? As you can easily see every one of these snapshots goes against what you might normally expect. Jesus and his Kingdom always move to the beat of a different drummer.

The second discipline emerges out of the first: **REFRAME YOUR WEAKNESSES**. To reframe your weaknesses is to deal with the wickedness factor in your life. **<u>Mourning means to develop a sensitivity to that which keeps you from being and doing all that you were created to be and to do</u>**. This discipline or attitude builds right on top of the first — it reaffirms your spiritual poverty. Once you have a right evaluation of yourself, God, and others, it is natural to be sensitive to anything that might pull you down or pull you away from being and doing what's right. It's mourning over that which keeps you from Jesus and his Kingdom.

You reframe your weaknesses by mourning — genuine mourning. By the way, when you mourn, you must feel the pain. Moan and groan over it! Feel it! Don't deny your feelings about it! The pain is for real, so really feel it! If you mourn properly, you'll discover something of a surprise on the other end. You will find a sense of comfort and inner joy.

 Want painful events have you mourned in your life so far? Did you eventually get through the pain and find some sense of comfort?

Fortunately, or unfortunately, you don't need to look for problems and troubles — either generated by you or delivered to you. They have already been "scheduled" for your endurance. One of the primary growth factors in life is developing your muscle of endurance. When you reframe your weaknesses, you set yourself up for greater growth. So, don't waste your sorrows, reframe them.

 What is it that keeps you from walking with Jesus and living the Kingdom lifestyle? What keeps you drifting away from what you know you really want with respect to your faithfulness to him? List it out and actually MOURN over it. There's something about identifying it and saying it that helps to push it out of your way.

NOTE one more thing within this snapshot. Jesus says, ***"Blessed are those who mourn, for they will be comforted."*** Focus on that second part: ***"for they will be comforted."*** You see, when you mourn over that which keeps you from God, Jesus says you will find an unusual comfort in the process. He will comfort you. This is what happened to the early disciples. Jesus was about to leave them. He told them that they were going to mourn over his departure. Then right away he said that he was going to send a comforter to them. He was going to send to them his Spirit to comfort them and encourage them. So, try it out. Reframe your weaknesses so that you turn them into mourning. Then, the Spirit of Jesus will comfort you himself. ***"Blessed are those who mourn, for they will be comforted."***

MEEK

We have considered the first two snapshots of what a Kingdom dweller looks like – poor in spirit and mourning. Each one has an action step in the form of a personal discipline.

Here is the third snapshot: ***"Blessed are the meek, for they will inherit the earth"*** (*Matthew 5:5, NIV*). The discipline of this one is <u>RENEW YOUR CONFIDENCE</u>. To renew your confidence means to develop a quiet, controlled strength. Remember, the right evaluation of yourself before God included your wickedness and your wonder. Mourning relates more to the wickedness or weakness factor. And now meekness relates to the wonder factor – the quiet, controlled confidence that comes from your Creator. <u>His mark of wonder is upon you.</u>

Once you see clearly who you really are, you are ready for growth. Then, if you are able to mourn over that which keeps you from growing, you actually graduate through this pile of problems. Now, you can't remain under the pile of mourning; you must gain inner strength as you emerge from the pile.

If you only learn how to mourn and remain there, you will be content to wallow in your weaknesses. Don't wallow in your sorrows. Mourn them. Recognize them. See them for what they are. And grow through them!

To renew your confidence is to focus on the product of what you can learn in the midst of your struggles. "Gentle" is the word for meekness. **Meekness is not weakness. It's developing a quiet, controlled inner strength or confidence that can only come from God's inside operation on your life.** <u>This is why we continue to speak of transformation or regeneration</u>. It's an inside job by Jesus, himself, in your life. You recognize your desperate need, you mourn over it, inviting the Lord to do his work in your life. He does his work in your heart and creates a wonderful inner confidence – an inner strength that empowers you to keep going, and to start over when necessary.

It's learning to "grow for it," no matter how rough or how tough life can be. <u>Again, it's not what happens to you, but how you handle what happens to you that matters most</u>. Renew your confidence and live your life – inside out and upside down – all in the rule or Kingdom of God.

The struggle here in renewing your confidence is to be diligent to find your inner strength in His work and not your own.

Are you sensitive to God's transformation in your heart? Are you sensing a little progress in building that inner confidence? Can you describe what that feels like?

NOTE ONE MORE THING: Jesus says the meek will inherit the earth. Whatever losses the person of meekness may seem to be experiencing here on this earth, Jesus gives an assurance that the meek will inherit it all. ***"Blessed are the meek, for they will inherit the earth."***

HUNGER & THIRST

As we make our way through the Beatitudes, which are really snapshots of what a Kingdom dweller looks like, we come now to the forth. So far we have discussed,

Blessed are the poor in spirit, for theirs is the kingdom of heaven.

Blessed are those who mourn, for they will be comforted.

Blessed are the meek, for they will inherit the earth.

What's interesting is that each of these first three snapshots speaks of where you lack. After practicing these three disciplines, you are pretty much emptied. You are ready for anything that will fill you up. This is precisely what the forth snapshot and correlating discipline will do. Check it out.

"Blessed are those who hunger and thirst for righteousness, for they shall be satisfied." (Matthew 5:6, NASB)

NOTE the strong terms here — hunger and thirst, not simply desiring something or making it a high priority. This is desperation — the kind of desperation that has a full understanding of its need for God, a desperate kind of mourning and an attitude of meekness. At this point of desperation you are ready for hungering and thirsting for righteousness — for anything that is right and pure and good.

The discipline for hungering and thirsting for righteousness is <u>REFOCUS YOUR HEART</u>. To refocus your heart is to develop a passion for filling up the hole in your soul. Everybody is passionately seeking inner satisfaction. This fourth attitude or discipline is a kind of hungering and thirsting for what you want in your innermost being.

"Righteousness" is right living. It's walking consistently with God's standard. Jesus is the Righteous One who walked most consistently with God's standard. In a very real sense, there is no other standard in the world. **God's standard for living life is the only one you were created to follow. All other standards are not standards at all, but scattered attempts to live life without God**. Many of these attempts are couched in what we know as RELIGION – religious systems of dos and don'ts to attain some level of approval by God – to reach some heavenly state and to avoid going to hell. Unfortunately, man's best attempts are like going to heaven on a six-foot ladder. The problem with this method is that the ladder can only go up six feet.

> *Hungering and thirsting for righteousness has nothing to do with a religious system, whether Muslim, Hindu, Buddhist, Jewish, or even Christian. All of these religious persuasions are cultural in nature and each one can find its meaning and highest desires in the person of Jesus. Hungering and thirsting for righteousness rests in a personal relationship with the Righteous One – Jesus, himself.*

NOTE what happens if you hunger and thirst this way: ***"for they who hunger and thirst for the Righteous One will be satisfied."*** The term "satisfied" is used to describe the fattening up of cattle – to fill them up so that they have no more wants. Do you want to find satisfaction in your soul? Then you must practice hungering and thirsting for Jesus every day! It's the only possible way to this kind of serenity and satisfaction. This is truly a refocusing of your heart!

 What have you hungered and thirsted for in your life? What have you wanted so much that you could "taste" it or that you would do anything to get it?

It's only when sensing your emptiness revealed within the first three snapshots that you have access to spiritual fullness. These are the quiet cravings – the hungering and thirsting – for spiritual things, for the inner satisfaction of your soul! <u>Hungering and thirsting is not simply making it a higher priority or something you feel you really ought to do, but to hunger and thirst as if your spiritual life depends on it</u>!

Refocus your heart every day, talking to Jesus, listening to him, and seeking to please him with your life throughout the day. Maybe you need to ask the simple question, "Jesus, what do you have for me to do today?" Believe me, that simple question can automatically refocus your heart.

 What are you presently doing to refocus your heart toward following Jesus?

These first four snapshots of "blessed" Kingdom living are necessary for cultivating who you are before God. It's the powerful, invisible matter of the heart that makes you salt-like – the salt of the earth!

YOU ARE THE **LIGHT** OF THE WORLD!

Salt and light are inextricably bound together.

Salt is the inner quality of light; light is the outer expression of salt. Salt is being; light is doing. **Salt is to be sensed; light is to be seen**! Let's examine how this plays out in our responses to Jesus' revolutionary call: "Follow me!"

"You are the light of the world. A town built on a hill cannot be hidden. Neither do people light a lamp and put it under a bowl. Instead they put it on its stand, and it gives light to everyone in the house. In the same way, let your light shine before others, that they may see your good deeds and glorify your Father in heaven." (Matthew 5:14-16, NIV)

Note again that Jesus says, *"You are the light of the world!"* Not that you might be or you could be. Salt has a powerful, invisible nature to it; light is more like the visible presence of God. <u>Salt must be sensed – light must be seen! Light counteracts darkness.</u>

<u>The visible presence of God consists of the essence of salt and the radiance of light</u>. It must be attractive and authentic! The core of this light can be found in loving your neighbor as yourself. We are beyond the point where mere talk – no matter how good – can make an impression. Demonstration is required. We must live what we talk, even in places where we cannot talk what we live. The test is reality – authenticity – the genuine!

Whereas salt included a warning against being good for nothing, light is used to show us how to be good for something. It is the outer or doing side of these two images used by Jesus. You are the salt of the earth and the light of the world; you are the invisible and visible presence of God on planet earth. Don't become tasteless salt. Don't cover up your light. <u>Allow Jesus to be sensed in you and seen in you</u>.

 What comes to mind when you think of yourself as being "light"?

A disciple – a learner and follower of Jesus – must make it his or her single-minded focus to be like Jesus as best he can. Simply put, <u>see and hear what Jesus does and do it</u>!

Jesus appointed two roles for his followers – to be salt and light. The first four snapshots or beatitudes are about your relationship before God. They are quite personal – poor in spirit, mourning, meekness, and hungering and thirsting for righteousness. These specify the role of being the salt of the earth.

The second four are internal qualities also before God regarding our relationships with others. These specify the role of being the light of the world. Each one extends out of another.

If you make two lists side by side with the first four on the left and the second four on the right, you will observe some fascinating things about the interrelationships within all eight snapshots.

NOTE that the left side of the chart has to do with the first four and each is expressing what it means to be into BEING – to be SALT. The list on the right has to do with the second four and each of these is expressing what it means to be into DOING – to be LIGHT.

SALT (Being)	LIGHT (Doing)
Poor in spirit	Merciful
Mourn	Pure in heart
Meek	Peacemaker
Hunger & thirst for righteousness	Rejoice in persecution

Also note that each of the BEING snapshots is the basis for the doing snapshots. In other words, each of the DOING snapshots emerges out of the BEING ones. In order to understand what it means to be merciful, it is helpful to define its source in being poor in spirit. This is the same for each of the DOING snapshots that we are about to discuss.

MERCIFUL

Now, let's move on to the fifth snapshot or beatitude. ***"Blessed are the merciful, for they will be shown mercy"*** *(Matthew 5:7, NIV).* The discipline here is <u>REACH OUT WITH COMPASSION</u>. To reach out with compassion is to treat everyone with grace and mercy. This means to identify with others' needs or plights in life in a compassionate way. Insert yourself into their shoes as best you can. Search for how you might best assist them. Initiate a positive effect toward the people in the world around you.

> *Remember, whatever energy you give out, you receive it back at that very moment. It's an interesting principle of life. When you give out something to another person, you receive it by the very act of giving it away. So, when you show mercy to someone, you feel this same mercy coming over you.*

Reaching out with compassion is a source of healing for those you touch and for yourself, so that everyone gets better. Don't forget, this is not just an action toward another person; it's an attitude that is most natural and present within the Kingdom lifestyle.

There is no way you will be able to REACH OUT WITH COMPASSION or be merciful without the dimension of being poor in spirit – to REAFFIRM YOUR POVERTY. <u>Being poor in spirit is a pre-requisite for being merciful to others</u>.

 If you were to be poor in spirit, how might this lead to a merciful heart?

Therefore, in order for you to be able to reach out with compassion you will do well to reaffirm your spiritual poverty. In other words, <u>if you want to check out how you can reach out with compassion more effectively, start with reaffirming your poverty</u>. Start with checking whether or not you are poor in spirit. This makes so much sense when you think about it. <u>It's very difficult to show compassion to another person when you are filled with pride and haughtiness</u>. On the other hand, when you are a person who has a right evaluation of yourself, God, and others, you are freed up to be able to show genuine compassion to others. <u>When you have received grace from God, it's much easier to give out mercy.</u>

Is it difficult for you to show mercy to other people? Then practice being "poor in spirit." If you understand your wickedness and wonder – your spiritual poverty before God and a right evaluation of yourself before God – then you are able to offer mercy to another. If you are so caught up in yourself, then you won't find it easy to extend mercy to another person at most any level. So, beginning with a sincere acknowledgment of your desperate need for God, reach out to all those around you with sincere compassion. And, you will receive it right back in the process. ***"Blessed are the merciful, for they will be shown mercy."***

 What gets in your way of showing mercy or compassion for another?

PURE IN HEART

The second four snapshots are about your heart relationship before God as you relate to others. The first one of these is, ***"Blessed are the merciful for they will be shown mercy."*** Remember, being merciful emerges out of being poor in spirit. Now we come to the sixth snapshot or beatitude. ***"Blessed are the pure in heart, for they will see God"*** (Matthew 5:8, NIV).

On the surface, being **"pure in heart"** doesn't appear to have much to do with the others. But when you check it out as this term is used in the Scriptures, it's clear that "pure in heart" is about being loyal, honest, and trustworthy as a friend. In the Proverbs it says, ***"the king's friend is pure in heart."*** Pure in heart is one who can be counted on at all times – a safe person to have on your team.

The discipline for "pure in heart" is <u>RELATE AS A FRIEND</u>. To relate as a friend is to develop relationships where there is trust and love! Where there is trust and love, there is affirmation. Don't relate to others as friends for their approval. You don't want to give anyone that much power. Only seek approval from your Creator – your Higher Power. With friends, you seek affirmation.

RELATE AS A FRIEND naturally merges out of REFRAME YOUR WEAKNESSES – to mourn over that which keeps you from God. If you are able to have a sensitivity to that which keeps you from God, you'll have a heart that is able to relate as a loyal, honest friend – to be pure in heart.

The discipline here is to determine not to live all alone in living your life. You need friends around you and you must be the one who has this discipline as an initiative for your own life. Be first in relating to another, not waiting for others to befriend you. But note how it emerges out of your mourning over that which keeps you from God. <u>Friendship begins in your heart</u>!

Everyone is in desperate need of the dynamic of friendship. Without a friendship you die. Life flows through it and death reigns without it.

 How are you doing in developing this discipline? What is it that tends to hold you back?

Make sure to live your life with trusted and loving friends. A friend is someone who knows the song in your heart and sings it back to you when you've forgotten the words. But there's one more dynamic I'd like to suggest. Turn your friends into "walking partners" as you walk your walk with Jesus. Learn to discuss and do things in the name of Jesus and in the spirit of his Kingdom in that relationship. This will deepen any friendship into a life partnership as you learn to do life together.

ONE MORE THING: The pure in heart are given a special reward for taking care of the heart. They will see God. Whatever else that means, it's clear that God puts a high premium on your heart. Want to see God? Then allow him to own your heart. ***"Blessed are the pure in heart, for they will see God."***

PEACEMAKER

We come now to the seventh snapshot or beatitude. It is, ***"Blessed are the peacemakers, for they will be called children of God"*** *(Matthew 5:9, NIV).* The discipline is <u>RESTORE PEACE</u>. To restore peace is to develop peace within your sphere of influence wherever possible. <u>To be a peacemaker requires that you make peace where there is no peace</u>. Search for trouble, distress, brokenness, and those who are living in pieces. You don't have to look too far. Listen to those around you. There is a great void out there – a great need to be understood. In fact, you probably won't have to search, just listen and be aware. This is a strategic discipline that carries with it the dynamic message of the Gospel (the Good News). <u>This is Jesus – peace where there is no peace</u>.

 Describe a time or place when you made peace between two people or two groups or between you and another person.

In order to restore peace, you must see the other person's strengths. This proves that you are listening and truly understand. Seek answers for what's best for this person. Do what you can do to promote peace making – love, trust, and forgiveness. The world around you is in such desperate need of experiencing inner peace. When I even casually mention forgiveness in a seminar session, I notice the light bulbs switching on throughout the audience. People are in great need for healing – for knowing inner peace.

 So, how can you help restore peace in the world around you? Can you identify what you can do specifically?

The pre-requisite of being a peacemaker is to renew your confidence – develop the attitude of meekness. Remember that meekness is a quiet, controlled inner strength. You don't have a chance to be a peacemaker without that quiet, controlled inner strength. You see, <u>without that attitude of meekness, you have the tendency to be a reactor to people and things rather than being proactive, which is what restoring peace requires. Meekness is the inner strength that allows you to be a peacemaker.</u> Restore peace and make people whole or remove yourself from this responsibility and leave the people around you in pieces. So, choose to restore peace.

ALSO NOTE the peacemaker will be called a child of God. This is what God does. He brings peace to the world at great cost to himself. When you are a peacemaker, you are like your Father in heaven.

"Blessed are the peacemakers, for they will be called children of God."

REJOICE IN PERSECUTION

We come now to the last snapshot:

"Blessed are those who have been persecuted for the sake of righteousness, for theirs is the kingdom of heaven. Blessed are you when people insult you and persecute you, and falsely say all kinds of evil against you because of Me. Rejoice and be glad, for your reward in heaven is great." (Matthew 5:11-12, NASB)

The discipline here is <u>REJOICE IN PERSECUTION</u>. To rejoice in persecution is to develop the big picture on all troubles – especially the stresses that others bring upon you. Life is full of stress and distress. Many of life's stresses are circumstantial.

NOTE the reason for persecution. It's that same word we saw earlier – righteousness. As you hunger and thirst for righteousness – being like Jesus (allowing him to live his life through you) – you will make people uncomfortable and they will pick away at you.

ALSO note the kinds of persecution mentioned here. It's insults, falsely saying all kinds of evil against you because of Jesus and the Kingdom lifestyle you are embracing. And when you note who it is who is doing the persecuting in the New Testament against the early followers of Jesus, you will quickly find that this kind of persecution comes from other religious people who are jealous and threatened.

When Jesus, the Righteous One, came to explain the love of God to mankind, his simple message was to present himself and the Gospel of the Kingdom. It didn't contain a system of dos and don'ts that normal religious groups do, so this made the religious people of the day uncomfortable enough to persecute him terribly to the point of putting him to death – to silence this simple one.

If you are simply walking with Jesus, walking with others, and waiting on Jesus to lead out in your life, you will face the same kind of criticism and backlash. Your simple faith will make others very uncomfortable – especially those who believe they have it all together, bolstered by their many theological and religious props. However, for those who are discontent, hurting, burdened down by all of the religiosities in the world, you will be a welcome sight – a bright light of hope.

Have you ever been personally attacked or criticized, even harmed, for something you said or did or for what you believe or for who you are?

The pre-requisite necessary for you to rejoice in persecution is to refocus your heart. Your passion for filling up the hole in your soul with simply Jesus – for genuine satisfaction and fulfillment in him – can set you up as a primary target for an onslaught of verbal persecution. When you begin to experience a sense of inner satisfaction and some level of fulfillment, you will find the jealousy and envy of others waiting to cut you down to their size – or lower!

Rejoicing in persecution is the attitude that is necessary to stand up against this verbal barrage. The attitude is to take a bigger view of it all. Those who are verbally attacking you are hurting deeply within themselves. What is most encouraging is that they have noticed something about you. You are growing up. You are beginning to find a personal satisfaction that sets you apart. Your response must be to redouble your efforts at refocusing your heart even more. You'll need it to truly rejoice in the midst of this kind of persecution. Keep on hungering and thirsting for that inner, spiritual satisfaction for your soul by walking with Jesus and walking with others. Then rejoice in persecution. This will drive your detractors nuts. Enjoy it.

 Why might someone become uncomfortable or even angry when you live your life following Jesus?

NOTE what is promised for those who rejoice in persecution. Jesus says, *"For theirs is the kingdom of heaven."* We saw that at the very beginning with *"Blessed are the poor in spirit, for theirs is the kingdom of heaven."* The first snapshot and the last – being poor in spirit and being persecuted for being like Jesus. It's like all eight Beatitudes are wrapped up in a package – all describing what a citizen of the Kingdom looks like. What a picture it is!

These eight disciplines or attitudes are taken directly from the first seminar that Jesus gave on the hillside of the Sea of Galilee. They all begin with *"Blessed,"* which means to be congratulated or to be filled with happiness. Take on these attitudes and make them your primary disciplines of life. Meditate on them and discover the great depth within them. They offer you the ingredients that will produce the most valuable and powerful spiritual riches you could ever experience.

Note that every one of these Beatitudes is different from your natural instincts. When you follow Jesus, you are walking to the beat of a different drummer. Spend lots of time meditating and referring back to these eight dynamics. Make them yours. Go back to them often. Maybe even memorize them and ask God to emblazon them on your soul.

Blessed are the poor in spirit. Blessed are those who mourn. Blessed are the meek. Blessed are those who hunger and thirst for righteousness. Blessed are the merciful. Blessed are the pure in heart. Blessed are the peacemakers. Blessed are those who rejoice in the midst of persecution.

Now that is a very different lifestyle – the Kingdom lifestyle, all unveiled by the King – Jesus. In a very real sense, these eight snapshots make up a collage of Jesus himself. So, to embrace these for yourself is to embrace Jesus and his Kingdom personally. Don't hesitate on this. <u>There are many treasures and secrets of the Kingdom that will enable you to make the rest of your life the best of your life.</u>

As you think back on these eight snapshots, which ones do you find most difficult to embrace?

Poor in spirit...

Mourning...

Meekness...

Hunger & Thirst for Righteousness...

Merciful...

Pure in heart...

Peacemaker...

Rejoice in persecution...

 How does Jesus move to a different drumbeat than the world?

THREE HABITS OF FOLLOWING JESUS!

Simply repeating an activity until you get it right makes HABITS!

If, continually and over a long time, you practice good deeds, you will form good habits. Good habits cultivated over a long time lead to the formation of good character. The human spirit is like a field that must be sowed, cultivated, and weeded if it is to bear a good crop. You can only develop good habits by constant practice; otherwise you will develop bad habits that become progressively more difficult to break. Therefore, good breeds more good, while evil breeds more evil.

 What are some of your current good habits? What are some of your not-so-good ones?

Watch your thoughts; they become words.

Watch your words; they become actions.

Watch your actions; they become habits.

Watch your habits; they become character.

Watch your character; it becomes your destiny.

In our world filled with corruption all around us, we desperately need to be and to build people of character. Following Jesus, the revolutionary, is the surest way to build your character. Jesus speaks to this in his story of two builders: ***"Therefore everyone who hears these words of Mine and acts on them, may be compared to a wise man who built his house on the rock. And the rain fell, and the floods came, and the winds blew and slammed against that house; and yet it did not fall, for it had been founded on the rock. Everyone who hears these words of Mine and does not act on them, will be like a foolish man who built his house on the sand. The rain fell, and the floods came, and the winds blew and slammed against that house; and it fell – and great was its fall"*** (*Matthew 7:24-27, NASB*).

 Both builders hear the same words, yet each one has a different result. What do the builders do (or not do) that makes the difference?

As a Jesus revolutionary it's vital to embrace three basic habits. It has been said that to develop a habit, you must do it for three weeks. If you do it everyday for six weeks, you'll own it as a part of your person and character.

Here's a great visual: "A trail through the mountains, if used, becomes a path in a short time, but, if unused, becomes blocked by grass in an equally short time."

HABIT #1 – Walking with Jesus

The first habit in the Jesus revolution is **WALKING WITH JESUS**. As a friend said, "It's like the announcement that is made on every flight. 'Put your oxygen mask on first and then help those around you.'" Walking with Jesus is just like that. You must put on your own oxygen mask – your personal relationship with Jesus. That's what comes first – always.

Walking with Jesus is being aware of his constant presence in your life through the Spirit of God indwelling each follower. It's being with him, hanging out with him, and being in constant dependence on his strength and his lead. In a very real sense, walking with Jesus is learning to count on him in your everyday life.

Walking with Jesus requires that you <u>learn to feed yourself</u> every day. There's not only one way to do this; there is a vast menu from which to choose. Let's suggest a few:

Walking with Jesus is simply talking with Jesus throughout your day.

- ✓ Ask Jesus whatever you want.
- ✓ Express your deepest longings.
- ✓ Share with Jesus your deepest pains and disappointments.
- ✓ After you talk with Jesus, wait and listen for an answer.

Walking with Jesus is simply listening to Jesus daily.

- ✓ Practice reading the Scriptures. Listen to the Spirit's voice.
  - Methodically read **Matthew, Mark, John, Luke,** and **Acts**.
  - Read the **Acts of Jesus**, a chapter per day, for 28 days.
  - Read the **Proverbs**, a chapter per day, for 31 days.
- ✓ Discover daily devotional tools. There are so many!
  - Choose those that lift up Jesus as life's focal point.
  - *Jesus Calling* is a great tool.
  - Daily blogs such as "**THE 180" at www.timtimmons.com.**
  - Look for the new **www.jesusconversation.com or www.jesusconvo.com,** filled with study and inspiration.
  - Inspiration from **www.tamratlayne.com.**
  - Inspiration from **www.timmonsmusic.com.**

Walking with Jesus is as simple as breathing.

- ✓ <u>Breathe in</u>. Take in some of the words of Jesus, himself.
- ✓ <u>Breathe out</u>. Talk to Jesus about your desires – your heart.
- ✓ <u>Pause</u>. Take note of your relationship long enough to take the time to listen.

Walking with Jesus is practicing devotion.

- ✓ <u>Devoted to imitate Jesus</u> – to walk, talk, love, and think like Jesus. The question to check this is "What did Jesus do?" (WDJD?). Follow him!
- ✓ <u>Devoted to consult with Jesus</u> regarding your personal, family, and professional decisions. The question to check this is "What would Jesus do?" (WWJD?). Think like him!
- ✓ <u>Devoted to converse with Jesus</u> throughout your day. Prayer is simply a conversation within your relationship with Jesus. The question to check this is "What is Jesus saying?" (WIJS?). Talk like him!
- ✓ <u>Devoted to community as Jesus was</u> – disciplining yourself to do life with a few others. The question to check this is "What is Jesus doing?" (WIJD?). Look for him!

What are some of the daily devotional tools that you might use?

 How would you respond to each of the four devotion practices?

Walking with Jesus is in response to God's great love for you. Oswald Chambers said, "No love of the natural heart is safe unless the human heart has been satisfied by God first." Embrace God's love for you and respond to it by practicing walking with Jesus at your side every day.

In simple terms, do what he says. No matter what he tells you to do and say, you just do it. Think of it this way: "If you pray for a car and God sends a jackass, ride it." It's signing off as king of your kingdom and making Jesus your King. Don't you love the bumper sticker that says, "Want to hear God laugh? Tell him your plans." To walk with Jesus is to be willing to let him give direction to your life.

What Jesus wants more than anything else is a personal relationship with you. Once Jesus resides in your heart of hearts by simply walking together, you will find yourself living a revolutionary life. The revolutionary life that Jesus offers is completely satisfying to you and most attractive to everyone else. It's like being a light.

The habit of walking with Jesus every day is the habit of opening your day with Jesus by praying, "Good morning, Jesus. What do you have for me today?"

What do you find most difficult for you to practice this habit of walking with Jesus?

HABIT #2 – Walking with Others

Let's now examine the second revolutionary habit: **WALKING WITH OTHERS.**

As always, Jesus is our example of this habit. When he began his ministry, he chose three to come alongside him – to be with him. He continued to spend most of his time with these three. This small group expanded to 12, then the 72, and then the 120. In fact, at one point there were up to 500 who were fairly close disciples of Jesus. I'm sure most everyone who followed Jesus felt close to him, yet he walked most of his time with a few.

The disciples were sent most of the time in teams of two. Sometimes there were more, but you just don't see them traveling or living alone. Walking with others provides a level of personal support that we all need.

There are, at least, four benefits:

FIRST: <u>Strength to do whatever may come in life</u>. There's something about knowing you are not alone that empowers whatever you try to do. Without others in your life you are weakened and at your lowest.

SECOND: <u>Encouragement is easily drained, yet within a few trusted friends you will find yourself fueled by the others who are doing life with you</u>. Without others you can easily become discouraged and distracted.

THIRD: <u>A learning dynamic presents itself within a smaller setting</u>. When you are walking with others, it's so much easier to get it – your seeing and hearing seem to be better. Without others it seems difficult to have ears to hear and eyes to see, so you just don't "get it."

FOURTH: Finally and most importantly, <u>walking with others is a sure place where Jesus will show up</u>. Without others you tend to forget how real and present Jesus is.

The experience of the early followers of Jesus is recorded in Acts 2: *"So then, those who had received his word were baptized; and that day there were added about thousand souls. They were <u>continually devoting themselves to the apostles' teaching</u> and <u>to fellowship</u>, <u>to the breaking of bread</u> and <u>to prayer</u>"* (verses 41-42, NASB).

The next verses tell us the results of gathering together in the name of Jesus were many:

(1) "Everyone kept feeling a sense of awe;" (2) "and many wonders and signs were taking place through the apostles." (3) "And all those who had believed were together, and had all things in common;" (4) "and they began selling their property and possessions and were sharing them with all, as anyone might have need." Radically valuing people over possessions! *(5) "Day by day continuing with one mind in the temple," (6) "and breaking bread from house to house," (7) "they were taking their meals together with gladness and sincerity of heart," (8) "praising God and (9) "having favor with all the people." (10) "And the Lord was adding to their number day by day those who were being saved."* (Acts 2:41-47, NASB)

WALKING WITH OTHERS is one of those disciplines of life that produces great results for you and those with whom you are walking. Jesus said, *"I will build my church"*; what he is looking for is for his followers to be the church, not go to church. The church is the gathering or assembling of those who are following Jesus. This is the Kingdom way of living your life fully.

Living fully requires that you walk with Jesus. <u>When you walk with Jesus, you are the walking solution to people's needs everywhere</u>. And the only way to faithfully walk with Jesus is to WALK TOGETHER!

Pray for someone to walk with as if you are on a mission together – and you are! People who are also interested in walking with Jesus more effectively are your best prospects, but pray for Jesus to open up these interested people to you. Focus on the following in your walk together:

a. Shine lifestyles together – the mission of lights to the world.

b. Sponsor love for one another.

c. Support blessing when insulted by others.

d. Share your stories of God at work in your lives.

e. Serve the needy around you.

This habit of walking together with others activates your personal transformation in Jesus and it also accelerates the transformation of the world around you.

What do you find is your greatest obstacle to walking with others?

 Can you think of a few others who might be good walking partners?

HABIT #3: Waiting on Jesus to Lead Out

It's not only waiting on Jesus to lead out, but waiting on Jesus to lead out with orders and opportunities. Learning this habit and really getting it is not so easy; it may be one of the toughest habit you will ever embrace. This requires the discipline of trust. You'll learn you must let go of the results and turn them over to Jesus, too.

Waiting on Jesus to lead out with orders and opportunities is tough, because you are no longer in charge of <u>what's</u> happening and <u>when</u> it's going to happen. You are forced to let it go, since you are not in charge. <u>All along you thought you were in charge of your life, but you are not</u>!

Waiting is not passive, but proactive.

- As you practice waiting, there is the <u>*action of readying yourself*</u>. Your responsibility is not to be in charge but to be ready for the King's orders.

- As you practice waiting, there is the <u>*action of relating to Jesus and to others*</u> — the first two habits. Your responsibility is to continue these relationships within your support team — the "one anothers" in your life. It's the doing of life together, not sitting around and explaining it.

- As you practice waiting, there is the <u>*action of resting*</u>. Your responsibility is to be anxious for nothing and to rest in your relationships with Jesus and with others. Now, <u>keep in mind that Jesus may not have direct orders for you today</u>. Don't be in a hurry to the point of being stressed. <u>Following Jesus is all about rest. Jesus calls his disciples into his rest — confident, peaceful, everything-is-going-to-be-okay rest</u>. The action of <u>resting is the act of trusting</u>. In some ways, this is like the athlete who prepares himself for the game, yet knows he must allow the game to come to him rather than pressing to make things happen.

 Is waiting or resting easy for you to do or do you become impatient or restless? Is it the same with waiting for Jesus?

We are waiting for Jesus to show up in our lives. We are waiting for Jesus to give us answers to our heart's cry — an impression, a peace, a desire, or a thought. We are to wait to bring restoration to those God brings us. We are to wait for God to bring people into our lives for us to walk with in fellowship and support.

Waiting on Jesus to lead out is demonstrating a ruthless trust in him to come through on our behalf with opportunities and orders for us to follow.

ONE DAY AT A TIME

Jesus said, **"Do not worry about tomorrow, for tomorrow will worry about itself. Each day has enough trouble of its own"** (Matthew 6:34, NIV).

Remember:
> Yesterday is a cancelled check.
> Tomorrow is a promissory note.
> <u>Today is the only cash you have.</u>

Many addiction recovery groups operate on the theme of "one day at a time." This is exactly what Jesus is saying here — one day at a time. Worry has little to do with the past; it mostly has to do with the future. We worry over what might happen or what might not happen. It's not in our control, but we spend lots of energy as if our worry could make a difference in the outcome. Jesus says, "Don't bother!" Each day has plenty of trouble of its own, so stop your worrying about or fearing tomorrow.

Just before Jesus articulates "one day at a time," he addresses two of the most common problems most of us face — worry and fear. What worries you, masters you. What you fear can paralyze you.

In Matthew's record Jesus offers the seeking of the Kingdom of God as an alternative to worry. He says, **"You of little faith! Do not worry then, saying, 'What will we eat?' or 'What will we drink?' or 'What will we wear for clothing?' For the Gentiles [or the rest of the world] eagerly seek all these things; for your heavenly Father knows that you need all these things. But seek first His kingdom and His righteousness, and all these things will be added to you. So do not worry about tomorrow; for tomorrow will care for itself. Each day has enough trouble of its own"** (Matthew 6:30-34, NASB).

NOTE there are two ways of living your life. Let's designate these two ways as earthly — the way the rest of the world lives — and heavenly — the way Jesus urges his followers to live. You could say the earthly way is the kingdom of man on earth and the heavenly way is the way of the Kingdom of God.

Jesus clearly describes the earthly kingdom of man as being filled with two dynamics. One: the nations of the world without faith eagerly seek after temporal things, such as eating, drinking, and clothing. Two: they continually worry about what they will eat, what they will drink, and what they will wear. The earthly kingdom of man focuses itself on this kind of stressing out; they spend their time worrying! Essentially, this is worrying about your life, literally your life's breath.

The Kingdom of God people of faith are given three instructions. **(1)** Know that God knows your needs and wants to provide them, so don't spend your time worrying about these things. **(2)** Keep on seeking after the Kingdom of God and God will add these temporal things to your life. **(3)** Don't worry about tomorrow either.

 So, do you tend to spend your time worrying about the earthly things of life and about what's going to happen in your future?

Jesus gives you the two-step answer to your worries right here.

Step #1: *"Stop your worrying, because God cares more than you do about your needs!"*

Step #2: *"Spend your time seeking after the Kingdom!"*

Focus your life and time on what it means for you to trust in Jesus enough to follow him. Focus your life and time on getting into a Kingdom state of mind. Look for the divine appointments God is setting up for you each day and do your best to show up! There is a watching, waiting, and worn-out world around you. They are in desperate need of answers and solutions that only Jesus can give them.

So, if you want to follow Jesus more closely and experience the Kingdom state of mind,
(1) Stop spending your time worrying about things the rest of the world is worrying about.
(2) Keep on seeking after the Kingdom 24/7.

In Luke's record Jesus offers the seeking of the Kingdom of God as an alternative to living a life of worry and fear. Jesus says, *"And do not seek what you will eat and what you will drink, and do not keep worrying. For all these things the nations of the world eagerly seek; but your Father knows that you need these things. But seek His kingdom, and these things will be added to you. Do not be afraid, little flock, for your Father has chosen gladly to give you the kingdom"* (Luke 12:29-32, NASB).

 How do you think seeking the Kingdom could have a direct effect upon your worries? Upon your fears?

Jesus repeats the same theme by saying, **"Do not keep worrying."** Then, Jesus warns of another problem that goes along with worry – FEAR. Jesus says, **"Do not be afraid, little flock, for your Father has chosen gladly to give you the kingdom."** Worry and fear are a destructive combination. Fear is the opposite of everything you are in your Creator, and therefore it has a negative effect on your mental and physical health. Fear is worry magnified.

If you find yourself eagerly holding on to either or both of these, you are living an earthly life without the benefits of God and his Kingdom. Jesus prayed, **"May your Kingdom come on earth as it is in heaven."** Jesus' answer to your worries and fears is, That's no way to live, so stop it and seek after the Kingdom state of mind.

Jesus teaches that if you are seeking his Kingdom and his righteousness, he will take care of everything else you need *(Matthew 6:33)*. He will do it one day at a time. This is what God did with the children of Israel about one month into their forty years of wandering. He rained down bread from heaven – manna – each day, except on the Sabbath. Each day the manna came down from heaven. Each day they were to gather enough for the day, never thinking of storing up some for tomorrow. Each day there was enough *(Exodus 16)*.

Jesus is the "new manna in town." Jesus is our daily bread. The word "manna" means a surprise, like "What is it?" Jesus gives each of us a surprise of his manna, his leadership, his sustenance, each and every day as we seek first his Kingdom and his righteousness. We practice these habits in order to gather the manna for today, which helps in minimizing our worry factor.

Have you noticed that when you think about tomorrow or next week, then the worries become overwhelming? You have to constantly refocus your thinking and reflection upon today.

- Walking with Jesus.
- Walking with others.
- Waiting on Jesus to lead out with orders and opportunities.

And do all of these ... *one day at a time.*

Which of the three habits do you find easiest? Which do you find the most difficult?

 If you disciplined yourself to have a single-minded focus on the Kingdom, what do you think your world would look like to you?

FIVE WAYS TO SHOW JESUS OFF!

LOOKING FOR THE INTERESTED...

Jesus shows up *"where two or three come together in his name."* When Jesus shows up, no one is the same again. The dead are brought back to life. The blind see. The lame walk. The deaf hear. The mute talk. Enemies and rivals become friends. Women's status is elevated. The poor are made rich. The rich realize their poverty. The lost are found. The weak find strength. The strong are made aware of their weakness.

No transformation is more vivid than what happened to the early disciples. Most were weak-willed and timid; they eventually found inner strength and courage. The usual reason given for this dramatic life-change is the resurrection of Jesus from the dead. The Resurrection is no doubt paramount, however their transformation seems to come from something else. After the Resurrection, it's recorded that Jesus spent 40 days with the disciples, where he spoke to them about the Kingdom of God.

Check out what Peter shared regarding that time, when he spoke to those gathered in the house of Cornelius: *"We are witnesses of everything he did in the country of the Jews and in Jerusalem. They killed him by hanging him on a cross, but God raised him from the dead on the third day and caused him to be seen. He was not seen by all the people, but by witnesses whom God had already chosen – by us who ate and drank with him after he rose from the dead. He commanded us to preach to the people and to testify that he is the one whom God appointed as judge of the living and the dead. All the prophets testify about him that everyone who believes in him receives forgiveness of sins through his name"* (Acts 10:39-43, NIV).

The real transformation the disciples experienced took place during this time spent with Jesus, eating and drinking and discussing principles of the Kingdom of God. And, this is the same today. When two or three are gathered together in the name of Jesus, he will show up and make a significant difference in all who experience him.

If Jesus brings positive transformation into every life he encounters, then doesn't it make sense for us to introduce Jesus to everyone who is interested? You see, when Jesus shows up, no one is ever the same again!

JESUS SHOWED UP IN THE BOOK OF ACTS

The active presence of Jesus is not limited to the 33 years of his life he spent from his birth in Bethlehem to his death and resurrection in Jerusalem. In the <u>book of Acts</u> Jesus continued to show up among his followers. It seems better to call the <u>book of Acts</u> the "Acts of Jesus" and not the "Acts of the Apostles."

Jesus showed up and the result was his followers sharing Jesus' message of the Kingdom to the world *(Acts 1)*. It was important that his followers knew Jesus personally, so he spent an additional 40 days with them with lots of personal interaction. Jesus apparently felt it was necessary to teach his early followers one thing – the Kingdom of God.

It was important that his followers understood the Kingdom, so during that 40 days hanging out with his followers the Kingdom was the subject of his teaching.

It was important that his followers had a strategy on how to take Jesus' message of the Kingdom throughout the world, so Jesus urged them to wait for his Spirit to come upon them to give them the power to spread this revolutionary message to the world.

Jesus showed up through Peter to communicate his message to many nations *(Acts 2)*. Jesus showed up through Peter and John to empower the healing of a lame man *(Acts 3)*. Jesus showed up to empower several articulate moments through his followers *(Acts 4, 5, and 7)*. Jesus showed up to apprehend Paul to bear his name everywhere outside of Jerusalem – to the house of Israel, to the non-Jewish nations of the world, and to their kings *(Acts 9)*. Jesus showed up to demonstrate to Peter that his message must not be contained within a Jewish box, but is for everyone everywhere *(Acts 10)*.

ACTS 29 – TODAY!

<u>Several of us who are walking together have found that reading the Acts of Jesus one chapter per day to be an amazing experience</u>. We have read it through for several months at a time and it increases our own awareness of when and where Jesus is showing up in our lives today. There are 28 chapters in the Acts of Jesus. We start on the 1st day of the month reading chapter 1 and then read a chapter a day according to the monthly calendar through the 28th day of the month. If you want to be more aware of Jesus sightings in your life, pick a month and begin reading through the Acts of Jesus.

It's important to note that Jesus' activity doesn't stop at the end of the 28th chapter. Jesus continues to act each and every day – 24 hours a day and 365 days a year. Therefore, we have found it most helpful to move into the rest of our lives with Jesus. We call it Acts 29!

Acts 29 is living out your relationship with Jesus today, because Jesus continues to act in and through all followers who have ears to hear and eyes to see. "When and where Jesus shows up" is not just a cliché or hope or mystical hysteria. It's a reality and we have been experiencing this reality for several years. The Jesus movement was launched when Jesus showed up among his followers and that transformational movement is still on today!

FIVE WAYS TO SHOW JESUS OFF

So, the "acts of Jesus" become powerful as we write Acts 29 through our lives. There seem to be five ways to communicate the Good News message of Jesus by what we do. These are ways to show Jesus off through our lives.

 So, as followers of Jesus, how can we best show Jesus off? How can we best lift Jesus up so people can see him without religious blinders? How can we advance the conversation of Jesus most effectively?

 In your experience, what have you been taught that works best?

Jesus said that many are interested in him, even interested enough to follow him *(John 4:35)*. We're looking for those who are interested. This is really the only requirement that is necessary – to be interested. Disciples of Jesus orbit around their world, looking for those who have ears to hear and eyes to see. You're not trying to close any spiritual deals or looking for people to preach to; you're looking for the interested! They are all around you.

Years ago *The Last Temptation of Christ* movie was released. At best, it was a bad movie and probably would not have lasted more than a couple of weeks in the theaters, but it was actually promoted by Christians. Because Christians organized against this movie with signs and angry demonstrations, they drew massive media attention to the demonstrators, which in turn attracted more people into the theaters to see the movie.

There was a lot to be learned through that experience. Jesus doesn't need or want demonstrations for him. Jesus wants his followers to be demonstrations of him – doing what Jesus would do and saying what he would say.

In order to demonstrate Jesus in your world, it's important to be like Jesus in all of your actions. We've discovered five specific ways to demonstrate him – to show Jesus off!

1. How you live your life. Jesus said, *"You are the light of the world. A town built on a hill cannot be hidden. Neither do people light a lamp and put it under a bowl. Instead they put it on its stand, and it gives light to everyone in the house. In the same way, let your light shine before others, that they may see your good deeds and glorify your Father in heaven"* *(Matthew 5:14-16, NIV).*

By this we see that it is possible for people to be attracted to God through your good deeds – your lifestyle. How you live your life speaks loudly to those who are watching. How you handle your problems and stresses, how you love your spouse, and how you treat your family and friends are all on display. People can see Jesus in this way!

By the way, no words need to be spoken by you here. It's not the fancy or spiritual talk, but the walk that matters most to people. People watch closely for that ethos – that credibility in your life. When they see it, then (and only then) do your words have any weight. So show Jesus off with your Jesus lifestyle!

It's interesting to note the feedback we frequently receive. It's not what we do so much as it is what we don't do. We don't enter into the world of gossip. We don't condemn others. We don't act like we have it together. We don't cover up our weaknesses and mistakes. We love both the powerful and the poor. We embrace the disenfranchised. We don't hesitate to serve when asked. This kind of down-to-earth, authentic lifestyle is so attractive. <u>This kind of lifestyle is Jesus</u>!

 What are some actions you can take that would communicate a message without using any words?

2. How you love one another. Jesus said, *"A new command I give you: Love one another. As I have loved you, so you must love one another. By this everyone will know that you are my disciples, if you love one another"* (John 13:34, NIV).

People can also see Jesus by your love for one another. This is so attractive and contagious. People all around you are desperate to love and be loved. Remember what we said earlier: <u>we are not in need of more love in the world, but more lovers</u>.

Jesus is reflected in this kind of love for one another. Jesus is not reflected in the divisiveness of the many religious communities that seem to compete and war against one another. It's ugly and it's devoid of the sacrificial love and the message Jesus came to bring. Jesus prayed that all those who follow him might be one – in unity with him. <u>Jesus unites; all else divides</u>. <u>So show Jesus off with your love for one another</u>!

 What are some of the ways you are able to demonstrate love to others?

3. How you respond to attacks. Consider these words from Peter, rooted in the ethics of the one who taught us to love our enemies. *"**All of you, be like-minded, be sympathetic, love one another, be compassionate and humble. Do not repay evil with evil or insult with insult. On the contrary, repay evil with blessing, because to this you were called so that you may inherit a blessing…. Always be prepared to give an answer to everyone who asks you to give the reason for the hope that you have"** (1 Peter 3:8-9,15, NIV).*

People who give a blessing when insulted are acting in a counter-cultural sort of way. It's moving to the beat of a different drummer in the name and spirit of Jesus.

When you bless someone who insults you, then people notice that you live your life differently from most everyone else who wants to get ahead or who wants to get even. Note that when you act this way, <u>those watching will ask you for the reason for your rare response to the insults sent your way</u>. This is a perfect time to share with those who ask about the Jesus way of life. So <u>show Jesus off by giving a blessing when you are insulted</u>!

 How do you think you might feel if you responded with kindness to someone who has insulted you? Would this be difficult to do?

4. What you tell others. The apostle Paul wrote, ***"But how can people call for help if they don't know who to trust? And how can they know who to trust if they haven't heard of the One who can be trusted? And how can they hear if nobody tells them? And how is anyone going to tell them, unless someone is sent to do it?"*** *(Romans 10:14-16, MSG).*

Using words – this, too, is one of the ways we show Jesus off. Note this is not you preaching to or arguing with anyone. The best thing to share is your own personal story. No one can argue with your own experience and the hope you have found through knowing and following Jesus. As we, Tamrat and Tim, share our experiences and share our stories, they are most powerful and credible. Tamrat's story is of Jesus finding him in political prison and Tim's story is of Jesus finding him in a religious prison! Don't be afraid to share your story. When you are a follower of Jesus, your story is really Jesus' story through you!

Jesus sent out his early followers without giving them a set speech or presentation. He took an entirely different approach. He promised them that they would be given what to say by his Spirit (*Matthew 10:19-20*). So, quit talking so much and start embracing Jesus as a lifestyle, learning how to love others, and then he will give you what to say, when you need it. Your Jesus story of transformation is beautiful and attractive!

 What are some of the times and places that you have shared your personal story?

5. How you take care of the needy. In Jesus' story about the sheep and the goats, the king welcomes the righteous into his Kingdom and commends them for taking care of him when he was needy. *" 'Lord,' they ask, 'when did we see you hungry and feed you, or thirsty and give you something to drink? And when did we see you a stranger and invite you in, or naked and clothe you? When did we see you sick or in prison and come to you?' To this the King answers, 'Truly I say to you, to the extent that you did it to one of these brothers of mine, even the least of them, you did it to me' "* (Matthew 25:37-40).

Here Jesus reveals another way that will have a most definite impact in the world and demonstrate the heart of Jesus. Being aware of Jesus' heart and recognizing that Jesus, himself, can be found in those in need in our world – the hungry, the thirsty, the naked, the stranger, the sick, and those in prison – shows off the sacrificial love message of Jesus in a dramatic way.

Jesus also spoke directly to those who didn't notice Jesus in the midst of the needy. The king in the story says to the wicked, *"Truly I tell you, whatever you did not do for one of the least of these, you did not do for me"* (Matthew 25:45, authors' paraphrase). When we are aware of the poor and needy around us, we are demonstrating the heart of Jesus in our world. Jesus always sought them out, and so should we. When we do, the attractiveness of the sacrificial love of Jesus shines through. Again, there may be no talking required here.

What are some of the ways you have done something for those people described in the passage above?

Our work locally in feeding and clothing the homeless is so simple, yet word gets out. People are fearful of being around the homeless. They don't know what to say or do. Most only see them in random encounters on street corners or outside a grocery store. When members of our little group were going regularly to feed the homeless, we made it a point to invite our friends to come along. What they found was one of the richest experiences ever!

They were able to interact with a homeless person and discover the real story behind the rags and bags. And when a person returned to help the homeless, the homeless remembered them. We used this field trip experience to teach what is on the heart of Jesus. Many who came along with us were members of some religious organization – Churches, Mosques, Temples. The Jesus friendships that were initially developed in serving the homeless are still very much alive today!

DIVINE APPOINTMENTS

Each of these actions shows Jesus off to the world – living a lifestyle like Jesus, loving one another, blessing when insulted, sharing your own story, and helping those in need. In fact, when you do these things, you are living a lifestyle on a different level altogether, and people notice. The people who notice are the people who are watching you day after day. This is Kingdom living at its core!

When you awake in the morning, try saying, "Good morning, Jesus! What do you have for me to do today?" With this greeting and question, you set out on a most amazing adventure – every day! Like everyone else, I have all kinds of appointments throughout my day. However, I am looking to see where Jesus might show up, whether in a scheduled appointment (where I know whom I'm meeting with and when it is), a spontaneous appointment (where I know the person but hadn't planned on seeing him today), or a surprise appointment (where I don't know the person and had no idea I might meet him).

I believe God is setting up divine appointments all day long just for you. He wants to love and touch people through you. He sets these appointments up! All he wants from you is for you to show up. Show up, and you'll be showing Jesus off at the same time.

 Can you see yourself embracing one of these five ways to show Jesus off this week?

THE FINISHED WORK OF JESUS

Throughout the world in Christian circles, there is a constant theme on the Friday before Easter Sunday. On this day, many Churches examine the seven words of Jesus on the cross or refer to them to some extent. One of these sayings of Jesus was **"It is finished."** If you were to survey most Christians and other religious groups today and ask them, "What is the finished work of Jesus that he came to accomplish?" you will receive the same answer most of the time. The finished work of Jesus was to die on the cross for the sins of the world. Jesus did come to die and he told this a few times to his disciples, but they just didn't get it or didn't want to get it.

As important as the death of Jesus is, Jesus gives a more specific reason why he came. Jesus specifically says what his work was that he came to accomplish in his prayer in John's gospel.

A few days before Jesus died on the cross, he revealed what his finished work actually was – the reason why he was sent to earth. So, what did Jesus say was the work he came to complete? When Jesus prayed to the Father, he prayed for himself, for his disciples, and for us today. This is the real Lord's Prayer. The "Our Father who art in heaven" prayer is better viewed as the disciples' prayer, when he was teaching the disciples to pray.

So, what was it that Jesus came to do? What is the work he came to complete? The finished work of Jesus is more than what we normally think. It's within these words of Jesus' prayer in John 17 that we can find the true revolutionary nature of what Jesus came to do and what he expects from us as disciples. Jesus said that he finished the work the Father sent him to do: **"I have brought you glory on earth by finishing the work you gave me to do"** *(John 17:4, NIV).*

Notice what Jesus says is the finished work he came to do. *"I glorified You on the earth, having accomplished [finished] the work which You have given Me to do.*

"I have manifested Your name to the men whom You gave Me out of the world; they were Yours and You gave them to Me, and they have kept Your word. Now they have come to know that everything You have given Me is from You; for the words which You gave Me I have given to them; and they received them and truly understood that I came forth from You, and they believed that You sent Me . . .

"But now I come to You; and these things I speak in the world so that they may have My joy made full in themselves. I have given them Your word." *(John 17:4,6-8,13-14, NASB)*

 From Jesus' words here, what would you say is the work that Jesus came to accomplish?

Jesus came into this world to invest his life in a few men and now he sends us out to do the same.

"As You sent Me into the world, I also have sent them into the world. For their sakes I sanctify Myself, that they themselves also may be sanctified in truth. I do not ask on behalf of these alone, but for those also who believe in Me through their word; that they may all be one; even as You, Father, are in Me and I in You, that they also may be in Us, so that the world may believe that You sent Me. The glory which You have given Me I have given to them, that they may be one, just as We are one; I in them and You in Me, that they may be perfected in unity, so that the world may know that You sent Me, and loved them, even as You have loved Me. . . . And I have made Your name known to them, and will make it known, so that the love with which You loved Me may be in them, and I in them." (John 17:18-23,26)

Jesus invested in a few — all those God brought to him. This is the finished work of Jesus. He invested in the Twelve and lost one of these, so he gave himself to eleven men. Now if this strategy was good enough for Jesus, then don't you think it's the best strategy for us as well?

Just as Jesus met and gave healing to one person at a time, so we are to do the same.

What are you doing with the people God has brought to you? Are you investing your life and teachings in these few? Jesus saw this work as the most important work ever. Don't you think we can take a clue from Jesus and do the same?

 If you were to follow this same strategy, who are the ones God has brought your way? What can you do to reveal Jesus to them?

JESUS UNITES, EVERYTHING ELSE DIVIDES

Jesus is the unity that overcomes all divisiveness! There is no alienation that cannot be reconciled by the introduction of Jesus. There is no debate, conflict, war, or class struggle that cannot be resolved by the introduction of Jesus. The message of the unity of Jesus is most revolutionary on most fronts within our various cultures.

In a gathering of highly motivated Millennial high school students who have been into a serious study of who Jesus is, their highest interest and attraction to Jesus is that people of all persuasions – religious, political, and philosophical – can find unity in Jesus. These students want to do something to change their world and believe they have a very good opportunity to do it. When they read the teachings of Jesus, they are more optimistic than ever!
Here's an example of what Jesus says about uniting the world, as he prays: *"I do not ask on behalf of these alone, but for those also who believe in Me through their word; that they may all be one; even as You, Father, are in Me and I in You, that they also may be in Us, so that the world may believe that You sent Me.*

"The glory which You have given Me I have given to them, <u>that they may be one, just as We are</u>
<u>*one; I in them and You in Me, that they may be perfected in unity, so that the world may know*</u>
<u>*that You sent Me, and loved them, even as You have loved Me*</u>*. Father, I desire that they also,*
whom You have given Me, be with Me where I am, so that they may see My glory which You
have given Me, for You loved Me before the foundation of the world.

"O righteous Father, although the world has not known You, yet I have known You; and these
have known that You sent Me; and <u>I have made Your name known to them, and will make it</u>
<u>*known, so that the love with which You loved Me may be in them, and I in them.*"</u>
(John 17:20-26, NASB)

This is the ultimate hope for our world! It isn't an educational, religious, or political hope; it's a person. His name is Jesus!

This is why we can have genuine fellowship with Muslims, Hindus, Jews, Buddhists, Christians, New Agers, Secularists, agnostics, and atheists. If anyone is willing to come together in the spirit and name of Jesus just to talk, there is a dynamic of unity present like no other you'll ever experience. We see this on a continual basis. This unity is occurring all over the world! We were recently invited to bring a delegation of non-Catholics to visit with Pope Francis and his leadership team at the Vatican. We met for nearly five days. The only discussion was Jesus and his unifying power. Jesus prayed in John 17 that all of his followers may be one and we are experiencing this amazing oneness in Jesus today. Jesus is unity! WHEN JESUS SHOWS UP, BEAUTIFUL THINGS HAPPEN, EVEN WITH PEOPLE FROM EVERY CULTURAL BACKGROUND ON EARTH!

WHAT CAN JESUS DO THAT NO ONE ELSE CAN DO?

What is it that Jesus can give you that you can't get on your own? This may sound a bit strange, but Jesus came as a revolutionary. The revolution is all about restoration and transformation.

For too long we believed we had the answers to everyone's needs and struggles. We didn't! The bottom line is we could only suggest some tools for them to help themselves. But, at best, these wonderful tools enable a person to achieve a level of reformation by reforming himself or herself. Certainly this is helpful, but reformation can only treat symptoms. Transformation is what is needed at the core level — an inner change of heart.

Since we've been following Jesus we have found four experiences that have become amazingly real to us and they come from the words of Jesus. And what is even more amazing is that through encountering Jesus, we are hearing these same experiences shared among those who are fighting the tough battles. They are fighting the experiences of betrayal, divorce, death of a loved one, fighting the ongoing treatment of cancer, international peace negotiations, and financial disasters. They are fighting in the military, families being torn apart. They are surviving the wearisome conflicts of others, along with a variety of addictions.

What is really needed is a genuine change of heart – to see your life, predicaments, and people differently. Several years ago, we set out to study only the five Gospels for three years – Matthew, Mark, Luke, John, and Acts. We did this in order to get to know this Jesus. This focus proved to be life changing! It was through this Jesus journey that we discovered what only Jesus can do for us that we cannot do for ourselves. We have no capability to change a person's heart. We can't give people peace. We can't give people joy. We can't give them love. We can't, but we've come to realize that Jesus can!

Again, we are not speaking of the religious Jesus. We are referring to the most prominent and powerful person ever! And, in the most pragmatic way, this Jesus seems to be able to affect these internal changes in people. Even though we have experienced this personally and have observed his effect in people who need what he has, we find ourselves caught up in the joy of actually seeing it happen.

There's something about Jesus without religious baggage – his words, his actions, his loving ways, his bent toward the disenfranchised, and especially his name – that brings healing and wholeness to the heart and mind. Jesus is truly the most effective person you can embrace for yourself.

Here are the four life-transforming experiences we are finding in Jesus:

WHEN JESUS SHOWS UP, THERE IS PEACE

The Experience of Peace. Jesus is all about peace. Peace is not just absence of conflict or a cessation of the battles waging in us and around us. It's a sense of inner calm that all is going to be all right.

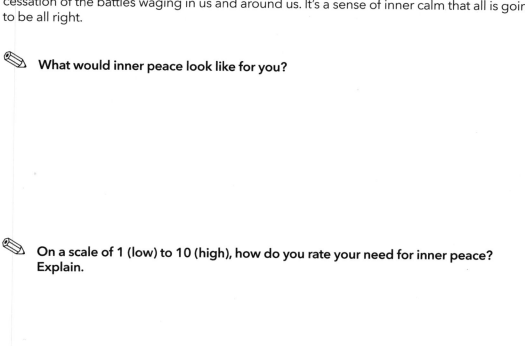 **What would inner peace look like for you?**

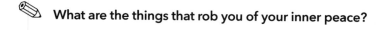 **On a scale of 1 (low) to 10 (high), how do you rate your need for inner peace? Explain.**

What are the things that rob you of your inner peace?

When Jesus first sent his disciples out, he sent them to go into villages and give the blessing of peace to those who were interested *(Matthew 10:12)*.

At the last gathering of Jesus' disciples before his death, Jesus said, ***"Peace I leave with you; My peace I give to you; not as the world gives do I give to you. Do not let your heart be troubled, nor let it be fearful"*** *(John 14:27, NASB)*.

"These things I have spoken to you, so that in Me you may have peace. In the world you have tribulation, but take courage; I have overcome the world" (John 16:33, NASB).

 Based on what Jesus says about peace, how can you receive the peace that Jesus provides?

After his death and resurrection, Jesus appears to his disciples and sets them up for a special mission. Jesus says, ***"Peace be with you! As the Father has sent me, I am sending you"*** *(John 20:21, NIV)*. As soon as Jesus says this he empowers them to go into the world and bring peace to everyone they meet. Jesus brought peace to everyone he met. Now he is sending out all of his followers to do the same – to be peacemakers – agents of reconciliation wherever they go.

 What does it mean to you to be an agent of peace? What makes this so difficult to do?

Through Jesus peace is available to anyone who wants it. This is the kind of peace that you just can't get on your own.

WHEN JESUS SHOWS UP, THERE IS JOY

The Experience of Joy. Joy is different from happiness. Joy is deeper than that. Happiness depends upon the happenings that are going on right now. Joy is an inner quality of seeing things with a positive perspective. Joy is the ability to enjoy the scenery, when you are on a detour!

"But the angel said to them, 'Do not be afraid; for behold, I bring you good news of great joy which will be for all the people.' " (Luke 2:10, NASB)

 What is the connection between Jesus' birth and joy? List as many observations as you can about Jesus and joy. How can you apply this to your life today?

Then, at that special final gathering with his disciples, Jesus makes an amazing statement about joy. *"I am the true vine, and My Father is the vinedresser. Every branch in Me that does not bear fruit, He takes away; and every branch that bears fruit, He prunes it so that it may bear more fruit. You are already clean because of the word, which I have spoken to you. Abide in Me, and I in you. As the branch cannot bear fruit of itself unless it abides in the vine, so neither can you unless you abide in Me. I am the vine, you are the branches; he who abides in Me and I in him, he bears much fruit, for apart from Me you can do nothing. If anyone does not abide in Me, he is thrown away as a branch and dries up; and they gather them, and cast them into the fire and they are burned. If you abide in Me, and My words abide in you, ask whatever you wish, and it will be done for you. My Father is glorified by this, that you bear much fruit, and so prove to be My disciples. Just as the Father has loved Me, I have also loved you; abide in My love. If you keep My commandments, you will abide in My love; just as I have kept My Father's commandments and abide in His love. These things I have spoken to you so that My joy may be in you, and that your joy may be made full." (John 15:1-11, NASB)*

What are the two things Jesus says about joy?

1.

2.

 What is it that Jesus spoke to his disciples that makes it possible to possess the joy of Jesus – full joy?

Jesus was teaching them about their relationship with him, that it is as vital as a branch connected to the vine. As a follower remains connected to Jesus, he will experience the same joy Jesus possessed. Think of it! You can have Jesus' joy in you in all its brimming fullness, spilling over into every area of your life and into the lives of others!

Jesus even challenged his followers by saying, *"Until now you have asked for nothing in My name; ask and you will receive, so that your joy may be made full"* (John 16:24, NASB). And as Jesus prays he says, *"But now I come to You; and these things I speak in the world so that they may have My joy made full in themselves"* (John 17:13, NASB).

Do you get the picture that Jesus is bent on his followers experiencing joy? Through Jesus, joy is available to anyone who wants it.

 What does this mean for you?

WHEN JESUS SHOWS UP, THERE IS LOVE

The Experience of Love. Although peace and joy are commonly identified with Jesus, love is the primary theme of who Jesus is and what he taught. Most Christian children know the song "Jesus loves me, this I know." Jesus is the epitome of love. To act like Jesus is to do the loving thing. Jesus taught that his followers ought to learn to be lovers.

"One of them, a lawyer, asked Him a question, testing Him, 'Teacher, which is the great commandment in the Law?' And He said to him, ' "You shall love the Lord your God with all your heart, and with all your soul, and with all your mind." This is the great and foremost commandment. The second is like it, "You shall love your neighbor as yourself." On these two commandments depend the whole Law and the Prophets.' " (Matthew 22:35-40, NASB)

 There are two dimensions to the greatest commandment. How do you see them working together?

There's something very fundamental about loving someone greater than your self — something of an inner balance that keeps you and your life in proper perspective. It's a centering effect!

In Jesus' prayer he shares how he sees his followers receiving and experiencing the love of God. *"I do not ask on behalf of these alone, but for those also who believe in Me through their word; that they may all be one; even as You, Father, are in Me and I in You, that they also may be in Us, so that the world may believe that You sent Me.*

"The glory which You have given Me I have given to them, that they may be one, just as We are one; I in them and You in Me, that they may be perfected in unity, so that the world may know that You sent Me, and loved them, even as You have loved Me. Father, I desire that they also, whom You have given Me, be with Me where I am, so that they may see My glory which You have given Me, for You loved Me before the foundation of the world. O righteous Father, although the world has not known You, yet I have known You; and these have known that You sent Me; and I have made Your name known to them, and will make it known, so that the love with which You loved Me may be in them, and I in them." (John 17:20-26, NASB)

As we have said many times, "We don't need more love; we need more lovers!" Jesus views our commitment to follow him within a loving relationship with God and within a community of other followers. He said,

"Just as the Father has loved Me, I have also loved you; abide in My love. If you keep My commandments, you will abide in My love; just as I have kept My Father's commandments and abide in His love. . . . This is My commandment, that you love one another, just as I have loved you." (John 15:9-10,12)

Keeping his commandments means to walk in his steps — to follow his example and teachings. This love relationship is so tight that a follower of Jesus can actually own the love of God in himself or herself.

Wow! As we read these teachings of Jesus, we wonder what went wrong. Jesus wants all of his followers to live in unity — to be one — to love one another. Yet, for the most part, we are divided. And worse, we are proud of it.

WHEN JESUS SHOWS UP, THERE IS GRACE

The Experience of Grace. Karma, which is another way of saying that we reap what we sow — is a reality. There are always consequences for our actions. But there is something that trumps karma — grace. Grace is something you don't deserve, something you didn't work for, something you weren't able to plan for or to orchestrate. Grace is given by Jesus, many times with no rhyme or reason to it.

Grace is one of the primary themes of Jesus as he touches the untouchable lepers and the unclean, as he opens the eyes of the blind, as he has compassion on the poor and the disenfranchised, as he receives those who are on the outside of the religious world, as he welcomes women and children — those normally pushed aside — and as he chooses the ordinary, uneducated to be the leaders of his movement. Just as grace trumps karma, so Jesus, the deliverer of grace, trumps everything!

"Therefore let it be known to you, brethren, that through Him forgiveness of sins is proclaimed to you, and through Him everyone who believes is freed from all things, from which you could not be freed through the Law of Moses." (Acts 13:38-39, NASB)

 What are the two powerful things that only Jesus can provide?

1.

2.

Which of these do you find most vital to your life?

 Which of these do you find most difficult to accept from Jesus?

Two of the dynamics within the experience of grace are forgiveness and freedom. It's hard to imagine two more powerful life principles than these. And these two dynamics are in tandem with one another.

Every time we bring up the subject of forgiveness, people immediately wake up and take notes. So many are locked up in a state of unforgiveness. Either they long to be forgiven for something they have done or not done or they are imprisoned by not being willing to forgive someone who has hurt them. Either way, people are stuck in a state of unforgiveness.

Once you forgive another person, you set a prisoner free. That prisoner is you. Once you experience forgiveness, either by forgiving or being forgiven, you enter into a wonderful sense of freedom.

Through Jesus, grace is available to anyone who wants it. This is the kind of grace that you just can't get on your own. All kinds of religious systems and programs offer you lots of things, but Jesus can give you true and lasting <u>peace</u>, <u>joy</u>, <u>love</u>, and <u>grace</u>.

Notes:

Notes:

Notes:

Notes:

WHY A JESUS CURRICULUM?

A curriculum is a progressive course of study.

There are 4 specific instances where a progressive course of study is mentioned around Jesus:

1. Jesus, on the road to Emmaus, had a progressive course of study in mind as he shared with the men: Then <u>beginning with Moses and with all the prophets, He explained to them the things concerning Himself in all the Scriptures.</u>

2. Jesus may have had an informal, progressive course of study in mind, when he said to make disciples by going, baptizing, and by <u>teaching them to observe all I commanded you.</u>

3. Jesus spent 40 days teaching his early disciples: **To these He also presented Himself alive after His suffering, by many convincing proofs, appearing to them over a** *period of* **forty days and** <u>**speaking of the things concerning the kingdom of God**</u>. In the same way Jesus taught the two disciples on the Emmaus Road in a systematic way, it seems to us what he felt was most important for them to understand about the Kingdom was a progressive course of study that took several days. It was a "boot camp!"

4. Even in *Acts 2:42:* They were continually devoting themselves to the <u>apostles' teaching</u> and to fellowship, to the breaking of bread and to prayer. We're convinced the apostle's teachings were the teachings of Jesus that each one shared.

The real need we know to be true is four-fold:

1. Too many friends who love Jesus and can parrot back the "right" answers to key questions, but may not have inhaled the transformation of Jesus yet.

2. There are hundreds, if not thousands, of small groups that continue to meet without any progressive course of study. They don't know what to do. They don't know there is so much more to embrace about Jesus and the Kingdom. There are even more potential groups that either haven't started to meet or began and faded away, because they don't know what to do. It's not enough to have information in hand; there is a great need to provide ways to advance the conversation of Jesus. **We believe disciples must not only know Jesus and his teachings, but must be conversant with what they know.** To be conversant is evidence that they have embraced Jesus for themselves.

3. In order to respond to the mandate of Jesus to make disciples of all nations, we are convinced the small group strategy is best. **Small group is the most effective vehicle for transformation and discipleship.**

4. There is no curriculum that revolves around simply Jesus. All others are infused with lots of religious clichés and an emphasis on conversion and membership. **THE WAY is primarily about Jesus and his Kingdom.** Neither Christianity nor any other religious system is the way; Jesus is, so we have disciplined ourselves to be only about Jesus — what he says and does.

Wherever we go, we advance the conversation of Jesus and leave small groups behind to continue the Jesus movement. **We encourage you to do the same, wherever you go.**

In addition to the websites of **www.tamratlayne.com** and **www.timtimmons.com**, be sure to check out **www.lifecenterethiopia.com**. This is a revolutionary model for loving and meeting the needs of orphans and widows, first in Ethiopia and then in the cities of the world.

Be on the lookout for a new and exciting website: **www.jesusconversation.com** and **www.jesusconvo.com**, where you can interact about everything Jesus, family, and the Jesus movement.